ENDORSEM

I'll tell you what, there are books, and then there is *a book*, and, ladies and gentlemen, what you hold in your hands right now is *that book!* Many years ago, my dear friend, Jerry Savelle, wrote *If Satan Can't Steal Your Joy, He Can't Keep Your Goods*, and I'm so excited that it's being relaunched to a new generation. This man had the vision and revelation of God about the power of joy when he wrote this book all those many years ago. It brought life, prosperity, and favor to those who read it and locked on to the truth of God's Word, and I have no doubt it will do the same for you. So, sit down, take some notes, have a good read, and share it with others. I highly recommend this book!

Jesse Duplantis
Evangelist, Author, TV Host
President and Founder of Jesse Duplantis Ministries

My wife and I have benefitted greatly from the ministry of Jerry Savelle since the 1970s. He is truly one of the pioneers of what is called "Word of Faith," which is not a movement but a timeless revelation. His teachings on faith and on favor are must-read, must-hear for those serious about overcoming and pleasing God.

In this book, he emphasizes that we don't have to allow ourselves to be stolen from. It is possible to resist fear and depression and to retain our joy, our strength, and our faith in the most trying of circumstances. Revelations like this don't age. They are just as powerful for future generations as when they were first preached to ours.

Let the truths in the book stir you to faith and victory again and again.

Keith Moore

Moore Life Ministries & Faith Life Church

For decades, my late husband Buddy Harrison and I shared vacations, ministry, and life with our dear friends, Jerry and Carolyn Savelle. We walked together through so many of life's trials and triumphs.

I remember the moment in 1982 when Jerry shared with us and our mutual friends, Happy and Jeannie Caldwell, a profound statement the Lord had spoken to him: "If the devil can't steal your joy, he can't keep your goods!" That revelation quickly became recognized as one of Jerry's signature messages. It was one that he didn't just preach to others—Jerry lived it without wavering. Jerry Savelle's joy-filled life always demonstrated the strength that the joy of the Lord brings through faith and love to secure the victory.

Today Jerry's message is more essential than ever. Regardless of what you may have lost or had taken from you, joy is the key to your enduring strength and restoration. The joy of the Lord will enable you to face and navigate any circumstance that threatens to steal your peace or crush your hope. I wholeheartedly endorse this book and encourage you to follow brother Jerry's guidance. Just as Jesus endured the cross by looking to the joy set before Him, you can inherit the victory that awaits *you* as you hold fast to joy!

Dr. Pat Harrison

Co-founder of Harrison House Publishers
Co-founder of Faith Christian Fellowship International
Tulsa, Oklahoma

As my friend for over 50 years, I still stand amazed at brother Jerry's anointing and ability to communicate to the reader the revelations that he receives from God.

If Satan Can't Steal Your Joy, He Can't Keep Your Goods is truly a classic and will continue to inform and inspire believers for generations to come.

I remember when the Lord gave this revelation to brother Jerry, and it certainly transformed my life.

Happy Caldwell

Founder and President, Victory Television Network
Little Rock, Arkansas

My long-time friend, Jerry Savelle, spent his life helping people to become the winners that God called them to be. In this powerful book, *If Satan Can't Steal Your Joy, He Can't Keep Your Goods*, Jerry shares time-tested truths that have helped countless people walk in confidence and victory in the midst of life's trials. As believers, we need to remember that the power inside us is greater than any of our troubles. Don't let the devil convince you otherwise!

Jerry had a great sense of humor, and you will see that through the pages of this teaching. Every believer needs a revelation of the Joy of the Lord. It will change your life. I know it did mine!

Richard Roberts
Richard Roberts Ministries
Tulsa, Oklahoma

I am so grateful for the revelations that the Lord has given to Jerry Savelle over the years. The great thing about what the Lord gives him is that they stick! *If Satan Can't Steal Your Joy, He Can't Keep Your Goods* is a phrase that is not only easy to remember, it is a powerful word that will completely alter any situation we face.

I have an original copy in my library and am thrilled for this new release to a new generation. They need to know how to maintain the force of joy in order to hold on to what the Lord has given to them.

Pastor George Pearsons
Eagle Mountain International Church

If Satan
CAN'T STEAL
Your JOY

He Can't Keep Your Goods

If Satan CAN'T STEAL *Your* JOY

He Can't Keep Your Goods

Jerry Savelle

CONTENTS

FOREWORD

Jerry picked me up in his $187.50, 1964 model 98 Oldsmobile one very cold morning, and I said, "Jerry, turn on the heater."

Jerry said, "Brother Copeland, it's on full blast."

So, I released my faith by shouting, "HEAT!" Then, I slapped the dashboard.

Heat came!

The joy came when Jerry said, "Slap it again; the transmission slips too!"

From that day on, Jerry would do the unexpected in our meetings by bringing joy everywhere we went—sharing stories and one-liners that cracked everyone up!

An example of Jerry's humor is the famous canoe story from his famous message, "The Law of Progression" (which can easily be watched online): "upstream, downstream, paddling as hard as he could," in his imaginary canoe.

In my mind's eye, along with everyone else, I could see the canoe and the paddle. After about the third or fourth time across the platform, everyone was laughing so hard no one could hang on to the worry, anxiety, and trouble the thief had placed on their hearts and minds.

Now we were all ready to receive what he was referring to in the refrigerator story (see page 7). It happened again, but it brought great joy and refuge in "the sweet by and by." It reminded me of the rest of the story, "But I need one in the rotten here and now!"

He bottom-lined it on page 9, saying: "The only reason I mention Satan's stealing is to make us aware of his devices so we can recognize them and overcome them instead of letting them keep us from victory and success."

Nehemiah 8:8-10 in the Amplified Bible, Classic Edition, says:

So they read from the Book of the Law of God distinctly, faithfully amplifying and giving the sense so that [the people] understood the reading.

And Nehemiah, who was the governor, and Ezra the priest and scribe, and the Levites who taught the people said to all of them, This day is holy to the Lord your God; mourn not nor weep. For all the people wept when they heard the words of the Law.

Then [Ezra] told them, Go your way, eat the fat, drink the sweet drink, and send portions to him for whom nothing is prepared; for this day is holy to our Lord. And be not grieved and depressed, for the joy of the Lord is your strength and stronghold.

The joy of the Lord, according to this First Covenant scripture, is the answer for grief and depression. In the Second Covenant book of Philippians, the apostle Paul writes to the church at Philippi. Despite being in some terrible conditions, Paul still tells the Philippians 19 times to rejoice!

Jesus said in John 16:22-24, *Amplified Bible, Classic Edition:*

So for the present you are also in sorrow (in distress and depressed); but I will see you again and [then] your hearts will rejoice, and no one can take from you your joy (gladness, delight).

And when that time comes, you will ask nothing of Me [you will need to ask Me no questions]. I assure you, most

*solemnly I tell you, that My Father will grant you what-
ever you ask in My Name [as presenting all that I AM].*

*Up to this time you have not asked a [single] thing
in My Name [as presenting all that I AM]; but now ask
and keep on asking and you will receive, so that your joy
(gladness, delight) may be full and complete.*

Carolyn, and all the Savelle family, are about the Master's (Jesus') business through the legacy of grace, joy, and
faith handed down by their patriarch, Jerry Savelle.

They walk by faith, and not by sight!

I know, I was there!

*But the fruit of the [Holy] Spirit [the work which His
presence within accomplishes] is love, joy (gladness), peace,
patience (an even temper, forbearance), kindness, goodness
(benevolence), faithfulness, gentleness (meekness, humil-
ity), self-control (self-restraint, continence). Against such
things there is no law [that can bring a charge].*

Galatians 5:22-23, AMPC

Kenneth Copeland
Founder of Kenneth Copeland Ministries

A SPECIAL MESSAGE FROM CAROLYN SAVELLE

It is such an honor to be sharing with you in this special edition of one of Jerry's most popular books, *If Satan Can't Steal Your Joy, He Can't Keep Your Goods*. My hope is that the stories Jerry shares in this book are as encouraging to you now as they were to us when we first experienced them.

In my opinion, joy is something that is sorely lacking in our world today. For most, joy is just a feeling, a sensation that is there one moment and gone the next. However, to God it is much more than that. To Him, joy is a fruit of the Spirit and the right of every believer to experience (Galatians 5:22-23; Romans 15:13). As we go about our lives, you and I must make the decision to not be moved by our physical senses. Regardless of the circumstances, we must give the Word first place in our lives. His Word is what we depend upon, and it's His Word that produces joy.

One of the greatest revelations Jerry and I received regarding this topic is that Satan could care less if you and I live or die; he is just a thief, who wants above all to steal the Word from us (John 10:10; Mark 4:15). Matthew 4:4 (NKJV) says, "Man shall not live by bread alone, but by every word that proceeds from the mouth of God." It's God's Word that gives us strength, joy, and the ability to achieve everything He has created us to be. That's why Satan fights so hard against us when we prioritize God's Word! One of his methods for stealing the Word from us is through adverse circumstances; if we give up in the midst of those circumstances we lose the foundation of the Word in us, which causes us to lose our joy. But if we stand strong and refuse to let go of the Word and God's promises, we'll have joy in every season! It gets even better: as Christians, we are entitled to make the devil pay us back seven times over, if we refuse to quit or let go of the Word, even when he steals from us (Proverbs 6:30–31)!

Jerry and I first learned this foundational truth in a story he shares later in this book. I don't want to spoil it, but it involves us, several trees, $3,000, and a very unkind man. When I think of this story, I remember the feeling of anger that began to rise in me after everything that had transpired. Jerry and I had been wronged, but it was our choice to either hold on to the anger we felt or choose to trust in God and walk in love. Thankfully, we went with the latter option, and that decision not only gave us favor for that situation shortly thereafter, but also planted the principle I am sharing with you right now deep within our hearts. When I think of that story, I don't think of what we lost; instead, I think of the joy we felt after we experienced the victory. Psalm 37:12-13 (NASB) says, "The wicked plots against the righteous and gnashes at him with his teeth. The Lord laughs at him, for He sees his day is coming." That day, God joined Jerry and I as we laughed at what the enemy failed to accomplish in our lives. I don't care what anyone says, if Satan can't steal your joy, he can't keep your goods! Keep the truths you read in this book in your mind and in your heart, and one day it will be you who is laughing as you reap the rewards of victory over the world.

Carolyn Savelle

Jerry Savelle Ministries International

Crowley, Texas

1

...HE CAN'T KEEP YOUR GOODS

Have you ever had anything stolen from you by the devil? Well, if you've ever had any contact with him, then he has undoubtedly stolen something from you at one time or another.

In the tenth chapter of John, Jesus said, "The thief cometh not, but for to steal, and to kill, and to destroy" (v. 10). We know that the thief He is referring to is Satan. Since Satan is a thief by nature, he steals. That is the nature of a thief.

Jesus says that Satan is a thief. Therefore, it shouldn't be uncommon for him to go around trying to steal things, nor should it be surprising to us that he does. He is after something. The Bible says he is after the Word in your heart (Mark 4:15). He is after your joy, your power, your peace, your courage, your faith, and your comfort. But not only that, he is after your goods.

One way Satan discourages many of God's people is through affliction and persecution. If that doesn't work, he attacks their material and physical possessions. He will attack their car, their finances, or their physical bodies.

We need to realize something about healing and divine health. Many people are struggling with healing because they see healing as something to be attained, something "out there somewhere" which they are trying to get. But, in reality, healing is not "out there somewhere." As far as God is concerned, we already have healing. It was given to us through the work of the Cross.

Divine health is something we already possess. When symptoms occur, it is nothing more than the thief trying to steal the health that is already ours.

In other words, divine health is not something we are trying to get from God; it is something the devil is trying to take away from us!

As long as people are trying to get health, they can't see themselves with it; and until they see themselves with it, they won't experience it.

Let me explain it this way. When the devil tries to put a symptom of sickness or disease on my body, I absolutely refuse to accept it.

A short time ago he tried to put symptoms of the flu on me. My nose and eyes started to run. I began to sneeze and ache all over. I haven't had the flu since 1969, and I'm not going to have it now. I'm redeemed from the flu!

Immediately I began to confess God's Word that I'm healed by the stripes of Jesus. I rebuked Satan and refused his lying symptoms. I wasn't trying to *get* something I didn't have; I was *keeping* something I already have. I *am* healed.

Those symptoms were an intimidation of the adversary. The thief was trying to steal one of my possessions—my health. I have health, and I stand protective over what is already mine.

Let me give you an example to illustrate my meaning. Suppose a stranger walked into your kitchen, loaded your refrigerator on a dolly, and started wheeling it out the door. What would you do? You would probably stop him.

You wouldn't start saying, "It certainly would be nice to have a refrigerator. One of these days, in the sweet by and by, I'm going to have a refrigerator." No, you already have a refrigerator, but somebody is trying to steal it.

No one in his right mind would open the door for a thief, stand there and watch his refrigerator being rolled away, then say, "You know, I remember when we used to have a refrigerator. One of these days, we'll have another one."

He is going to step in front of that thief and say, in no uncertain terms, "Where do you think you're going with my refrigerator? Get your hands off my property and get out of here!" He wouldn't be trying to *get* a refrigerator; he would be *keeping* the one he has.

So it is with healing. I am healed. When symptoms come, I just brace myself and tell the devil, "Hold it right there, bud! In the name of Jesus Christ, that's as far as you go. You're not getting my health. I'm healed, and you're not going to steal my health! Get out of here—*now!*"

I've learned to do this where my money is concerned, too. Have you ever believed God for a hundred dollars to pay off a note? Then when you got it, the car broke down. You had to spend the hundred dollars to get it fixed—and you still didn't pay off the note.

Do you know why that sort of thing happens? Because the devil is trying to steal our money. He's a thief. As Jesus said, "He comes to steal, to kill, and to destroy." If he is a thief, we shouldn't be surprised that he tries to steal from us.

In this study, I don't want to major on stealing. The message I have to share with you is not negative; it is positive. The only reason I mention Satan's stealing is to make us aware of his devices so we can recognize them and overcome them instead of letting them keep us from victory and success.

To defeat the devil and live the abundant life, you need to know how Satan operates. The apostle Paul said, "Lest Satan should get an advantage of us: for we are not ignorant of his devices" (2 Cor. 2:11). Satan has the advantage over people who don't understand how he operates. Once we are aware of his intentions and his methods, we should not major on the devil or demons. Let's major on the victory that is ours in Christ Jesus.

SATAN STEALS THE WORD

But call to remembrance the former days, in which, after ye were illuminated, ye endured a great fight of afflictions; partly, whilst ye were made a gazingstock both by reproaches and afflictions; and partly, whilst ye became companions of them that were so used.

For ye had compassion of me in my bonds, and took joyfully the spoiling of your goods, knowing in yourselves that ye have in heaven a better and an enduring substance.

Cast not away therefore your confidence, which hath great recompence of reward. For ye have need of patience, that, after ye have done the will of God, ye might receive the promise. For yet a little while, and he that shall come will come, and will not tarry.

Now the just shall live by faith: but if any man draw back, my soul shall have no pleasure in him. But we are not of them who draw back unto perdition; but of them that believe to the saving of the soul.

Hebrews 10:32-39

Notice verse 32 once again: "But call to remembrance the former days, in which, after ye were illuminated [or "enlightened," NASB], ye endured a great fight of afflictions." When you receive the Word, you are illuminated or enlightened. Psalm 119:130 says, "The entrance of thy words giveth light." When the Word enters your heart, it gives light; you are illuminated and enlightened.

Did you notice that once you receive the Word, the war is on? People have told me, "Dear God, I was doing all right until I got turned on to the Word." No, they weren't doing all right. They just thought they were.

Did you notice that after you got some Word in you, you had to stand in faith for that Word? Remember what Jesus said in Mark 4:15? He said that once the Word is sown in a man's heart, Satan comes immediately to take it away. Satan is a thief; he takes things away. Once the Word is sown, Satan "cometh immediately" to take it away.

The writer of Hebrews reminds them that "after ye were illuminated [by the Word], ye endured a great fight of afflictions" (Heb. 10:32). In Mark 4:17, Jesus spoke of those who "have no root in themselves, and so endure but for a time: afterward, when affliction or persecution ariseth for the word's sake, immediately they are offended."

Why did the affliction or persecution arise? *For the Word's sake!*

Satan is after the Word in your heart. You are no threat to him until you get God's Word in your heart. Then you become dangerous to him. Why? Because the Word of God is the power of God. The apostle Paul said, "For I am not ashamed of the gospel of Christ: for it is the power of God unto salvation" (Rom. 1:16). *When you get God's Word in your heart, you get God's power in your life.* It's the power of God that stops Satan's operation, and he's clever enough to realize that.

The devil didn't bother me much before I got saved. Sure, he controlled my life, but he didn't have to worry about me getting healed or about me speaking in tongues. I hadn't heard about those things.

Before I found out what God's Word said about prosperity, I just figured, "You win a few; you lose a few. What will be, will be. If you're broke, you're broke; if you're not, you're not. The rich get richer, and the poor get poorer. That's just the way the cookie crumbles."

One day I discovered 3 John 2: "Beloved, I wish above all things that thou mayest prosper and be in health, even as thy soul prospereth." The day I learned that, the light was turned on inside me. I was illuminated or enlightened. I had discovered that it was God's will that I prosper. So I prepared to prosper. Then it seemed that my finances were attacked harder than ever before. All I had done was to find one verse!

When I found out I had a right to prosper, what happened? My car blew up! That old clunker I was driving had over 100,000 miles on it. It was a total wreck. Before I went into the ministry, I was an auto body repairman. I had never owned a car that had not been "totaled out" first. Every car I had driven in my life had been wrecked and rebuilt.

My dad gave me the first car I owned. It was a 1929 Model A coupe that had been wrecked and reworked. I went from a '29 model to a '32 model to a '49 model, and so on. All of them had been wrecked.

When I graduated from high school, I didn't want to be an accountant, a businessman, or a lawyer. I wanted to be a "fender bender." My whole life was automobiles, and that was the career I wanted.

I was a hot-rodder. I love fast cars. Even when Carolyn and I married, I still drove clunkers. I put Carolyn in a '55 Chevy with a hot engine when she only knew how to drive a 6-cylinder. There were times that I would find her out on the road somewhere with the hood up, looking. She had no idea what to do to fix it. She would just stand and look at the motor. Then she started carrying a hammer around with her. When the car would break down, she would just start beating on the engine. But what should I have expected?

When I left the automotive business in 1969 and started preparing for the ministry, I was driving a '64 Oldsmobile 98 that was a wreck. I had paid $187.50 for it and rebuilt it. You couldn't tell by looking that it had been wrecked, but it had 100,000 miles on it when I bought it. The transmission slipped and the engine clattered. But it sure was pretty! After all, I was a body man, not a mechanic.

Then one night I found out that, as a child of God, I had a right to prosper. When that truth was revealed in my heart, Carolyn and I joined hands and prayed for abundance. We prayed: "Father, in the name of Jesus, Your Word says You desire that we prosper. Your Word says You open up Your hand and fulfill the desire of every living thing, that You supply all our need. We have need of a better automobile, so we believe we receive it."

Immediately after we prayed that prayer, our faith was tested.

A former employer called and asked me to come see him, so I drove my car to his place of business. As I was sharing my testimony with him, it was like the words of King Agrippa to Paul: "Almost thou persuadest me to be a Christian" (Acts 26:28). That's how it was with this man. Though I had captured him with my testimony, he wasn't quite ready to make a commitment. But he was pleased with all the good things God was doing for me.

As we left his office together, he followed me to my car, and I sat in it telling him about the abundant life in Christ Jesus. Then I cranked it up and started to back out. Before I could get out of the driveway, the thing blew up and caught on fire! What a wonderful testimony of the abundant life!

Satan came immediately to steal the Word. The first thought I had was exactly what the devil wanted me to think, *This stuff doesn't work!* Then I thought, *If I was Oral Roberts, it would work, but I'm Jerry Savelle. It works for Kenneth Copeland, but I'm not Kenneth Copeland.*

There I was, minding my own business, when my car blew up. Why? All I did was find out I had a right to prosper. You know, it seemed to me that Satan should have blown up God's chariot instead of my car. But the devil blew up my car and put me out of commission. They towed the thing to my house and set it in the carport. That was it; that was all I had to drive.

Now in a situation like that, what do you do? I wanted to take my Bible, throw it out the window—along with all those Kenneth Copeland tapes—and go back to beating fenders, drinking beer, smoking cigarettes, and going to hell!

Then I thought, *Now, wait a minute. I've missed it somewhere.* That's when I found out in Mark chapter 4 that Satan comes *immediately* to steal the Word. I discovered that "affliction or persecution ariseth for the word's sake" (v. 17).

I thought it was a personal thing Satan had against me. It wasn't. He doesn't care anything about you or me. It's the Word in us that he hates and fears.

I heard Kenneth Copeland make a statement years ago, and it went off in my heart. He said, "The devil doesn't care whether you live or die. In fact, it would please him if you would just die right now and go on to heaven. Then you would be out of his way."

That's right. You're not much of a threat to Satan in heaven. You're out of the way then. It's while you're here on earth with the Word churning in your heart that you give the devil fits.

You see, we've always had an image of the devil going around giving *us* fits. He *is* a worthy opponent, and he *does* come to steal, to kill, and to destroy; but it's time the Body of Christ started giving *him* fits! It's time we rise up and take our rightful place. It's time we determine in our hearts that the devil isn't going to steal the Word out of us, but every time he intimidates us, we are going to intimidate him.

I found out that Satan will come to get the Word. He will try to steal the Word out of my heart. I learned that affliction and persecution arise for the Word's sake. I discovered that I had received a revelation from God, and that revelation made me dangerous. You can see that it was to Satan's advantage to attack me immediately, to do anything he could to cripple me financially so I would begin to think, *This just doesn't work.*

It was Satan's idea that I throw my Bible out the window. It was his suggestion that I go back to being just one of those "normal" Christians, careful not to get too far off into this "faith stuff."

FOR THE WORD'S SAKE

Let's look at what Paul says again: "After ye were illuminated [or "enlightened"], ye endured a great fight of afflictions" (Heb. 10:32). He is telling us here what Jesus said: "that afflictions come for the Word's sake." After you have received revelation from the Word of God, the fight is on. You are engaged in warfare.

I'm not saying this to frighten you. I'm not emphasizing this fact so you will walk around thinking, *Oh, my God, what am I going to do when the afflictions come?* I am simply making you aware that we have an enemy, an enemy that will oppose us.

God tells us in His Word that His people are destroyed because of a lack of knowledge (Hos. 4:6). If you don't know how the devil operates, then you'll be one of those who blame God for what the devil is doing. You need to know that God is not sending those trials to teach you a lesson. God is not killing your cattle, wrecking your vehicles, or striking your family with disease "to teach you something."

When the devil cut off my baby's fingers in 1969, Christians actually told me God did that to teach me something. I don't serve a God who cuts off a baby's fingers to teach lessons. If He wanted to teach *me* something, why didn't He cut off *my* fingers? I used to serve a god like that—the devil—but I got delivered from his power. Now I serve a God of love. *My God is a deliverer, not a destroyer.*

Someone may ask, "Don't you believe in the wrath of God?" I certainly do, but I'll never experience it because I'm His child. If you are God's child, you won't experience His wrath either. His wrath is reserved for His enemies, not for His own children.

A PUBLIC SPECTACLE

After ye were illuminated, ye endured a great fight of afflictions; partly, whilst ye were made a gazingstock both by reproaches and afflictions; and partly, whilst ye became companions of them that were so used.

Hebrews 10:32-33

Do you know what a *gazingstock* is? *The Twentieth Century New Testament* translates it as "a public spectacle."

Since you made a decision to live by God's Word, have you ever felt like you suddenly became a public spectacle?

Does it sometimes seem that everybody is watching you—that you're on trial and you'd better perform?

Many times a wife will get turned on to the Word before her husband. He just stands by scowling and thinking, *I don't know if this stuff works or not. We'll just see. If she gets that new refrigerator by faith, then I'll believe.* He has put his wife and God's Word on trial.

Before I got turned on to God, Carolyn would ask me to go to church with her. I didn't like church, I didn't like preachers, and I didn't care who knew it!

When Kenneth Copeland came to town for a series of meetings, she begged me to go with her. "Jerry, please go. I promise you, this man's not like all the rest."

"Carolyn, you told me the same thing about the last 17 preachers, and you lied 17 times! I'm not going to hear this Copeland fellow."

So she went by herself. When she came home from those meetings, I could tell something was different about her, but I wouldn't let her know it. She would say, "Jerry, please, just come to one meeting and see for yourself."

"Carolyn, I did that the last time. Every time I go, you have told the preacher about me, so he picks me out of the audience and tells me things I don't want to hear."

She said, "I've never told those preachers anything about you!"

"You had to. How else would they know those things?" (At that time, I had no knowledge of spiritual gifts, so all I could think was that Carolyn had told them about me.)

It never failed. It happened in every meeting I would go to. It was as if I was waving a red flag. As soon as the preacher finished his sermon, he would pick me out of the congregation, call me up front, and tell me what all the others had told me: "You're going to preach."

I was convinced that Carolyn was putting them up to it. I would storm out of that church, saying, "I'm never going back. Those guys are crazy. I'm not preaching, and you're not getting me in that church again!"

But during Copeland's meeting, she became a new woman. I knew something had happened to her. She had received the Word and been delivered of that religious spirit she had been bound up in. She begged me again, "Jerry, this is the last service. Please go with me." Finally, she talked me into going.

I sat on the last row with my mind made up that I wasn't going to listen to anything this guy had to say. But for the first time, my wife had told the truth. Kenneth

Copeland wasn't like the rest of them. I had never seen anyone like him. I thought he was a smart aleck at first.

The first thing he did shocked me. After the choir had sung for a while, he got up and said, "All those songs you people sang tonight were embalmed with unbelief."

I thought to myself, *How can he say such a thing?* But he was right!

The next thing he said was, "Where's Brother Herb?"

Someone answered, "He's at home."

Copeland boomed, "At home? I told you to have him in the service tonight! God's going to heal him. Go get him!"

About three guys jumped out of their seats and left. Then Copeland turned to the congregation and said, "Open your Bibles," and he started preaching.

Well, he got my attention. I didn't intend to listen, but I couldn't help it after that. I didn't know what the guy was going to do next.

Boy, could he preach! The title of the sermon was "The Word of Faith." I never will forget it. He preached about how David took faith in his covenant with God and slew Goliath. Just as he reached the part where Goliath is beheaded, in walk these three guys carrying some fellow like a baby. They put him down about three rows in front of me, and I could see that he was paralyzed from the neck down.

As soon as they let go of the man, Brother Copeland jumped off the platform, ran up to him, pointed his finger at him, and said, "You devil, come out of him in the name of Jesus!" He grabbed him by the hand, jerked him off the pew, and ran around the church with him. That man took off and outran Brother Copeland!

Needless to say, from then on Kenneth Copeland had my undivided attention. What really got my attention was his honesty and boldness. For the first time in my life, I saw a preacher who made no apologies for being a Christian. He wasn't a smart aleck; he was just very bold in what he believed and dared to act on it.

The message he preached changed my life. At three o'clock one morning, I made Jesus Christ the Lord of my life, got filled with the Holy Ghost, and accepted the call to ministry.

I started studying the Word, and that's when the devil came at me from every angle. I felt like a public spectacle—like all the people who had been praying for me were standing back, hoping I'd fail.

Have you ever felt that way? Has it ever seemed to you that some of your closest friends, some of the people you grew up with in the Lord, were just standing back, thinking, *When he doesn't get the car he's believing for, then it'll prove that faith stuff doesn't work.*

Satan doesn't play fair. Paul says you are made a gazingstock—a public spectacle.

THE WORD PRODUCES JOY

For ye had compassion of me in my bonds, and took joyfully the spoiling of your goods.

Hebrews 10:34

"Took joyfully the spoiling of your goods." God used this phrase to get my attention concerning this subject. We had just concluded the annual board of directors meeting of our ministry. Board members had come from throughout the United States, and we had been together for a weekend, discussing the affairs of the ministry and fellowshipping together. It was a great time in the Lord.

After they had left, I was up late that night. About one o'clock in the morning as I was meditating on the Word,

I started reading this passage. Suddenly, that phrase captured my attention: "took joyfully the spoiling of your goods." I thought, *Lord, are You saying these people actually took joyfully the spoiling of their goods? That's unheard of.*

You see, the word *spoil* means "to seize, to snatch away, to capture, to take captive." Can you imagine anyone being joyful about losing his goods to the devil? As I studied this, the Spirit of God began to run Scriptures across my mind. I was so excited I couldn't go to bed. God began to teach me how to get back into my possession all the things Satan had stolen from me.

This is what the Lord told me: "Son, when you receive the Word, Satan comes immediately to steal that Word. Do you realize what the Word actually produces?"

The Word produces many things. In John 15:7, Jesus was talking about the power of prayer. He said, "If ye abide in me, and my words abide in you, ye shall ask what ye will, and it shall be done unto you."

Now that's good news, isn't it? If the Word of God abides in you and you abide in Christ, you can ask whatever you will and it will be done for you by the Father in heaven. Jesus goes on to talk about how God is glorified when we bear much fruit (v. 8). The last thing He says is this: "These things have I spoken unto you, that my joy might remain in you, and that your joy might be full" (v. 11).

The Lord said to me: "When I speak, My words produce joy. My Word is good news, and good news always produces joy."

It is good news to know that you can ask the Father whatever you will and He will give it to you, if you are abiding in Him and His Words are abiding in you.

In John 16:24, Jesus told His disciples: "Hitherto have ye asked nothing in my name: ask, and ye shall receive, that your joy may be full." In other words, He is saying, "You're not going to have to get things secondhand anymore. You're going to have the same kind of standing with God that I do." He was telling us, "My name carries weight with the Father; and whatever you ask Him in My name, He will give you so that your joy will be full."

Jesus said that the Word produces joy. When I found out I was healed by the stripes of Jesus, I got joyful. When I learned that I have a right to prosper, I got joyful. When I discovered that if I am a tither, God will open the windows of heaven and flood me with His blessings, I got joyful. *God's Word produces joy!*

Jesus said that when the devil comes to steal the Word, not only is he trying to get the Word, he is trying to steal your joy. If the Word is in you and the Word produces joy, then Satan can steal your joy by getting the Word out of you.

As long as things are going well, it's not hard to be joyful. In an atmosphere where there is the anointing of God, the peace of God, and the liberty of the Holy Spirit, it is no problem to worship the Lord. But then a crisis arises. Things get troubled, and everything starts going contrary to what the Word says. When that happens, there is an opportunity for your joy to be stolen from you. This is when the test comes. Faith is not tested *in church;* it's tested *in a crunch!*

Here is what the Lord told me. Remember this phrase: *"Son, if Satan can't steal your joy, he can't keep your goods."*

SATAN WANTS TO STEAL OUR JOY

Notice again what Paul said about the Hebrew people: Even though Satan had stolen their goods, they had taken joyfully the spoiling of those goods. The important thing was not that Satan had stolen from them; it was their attitude about his thievery.

Satan is a thief by nature. He will try to steal the Word right out of your heart. He will try to steal your finances, your health, your kids, anything he can to get you discouraged, sidetracked, and defeated. But if Satan can't get your joy, he can't totally defeat you. He can strip you of everything you own, but if he can't get your joy, he can't win!

You can't beat a joyful believer. The Bible says, "The joy of the Lord is your strength" (Neh. 8:10). If Satan were able to strip you of every earthly possession, every material blessing, you would still have the victory because you have the joy of the Lord inside you and that joy will strengthen you. If Satan can't get your joy, he can't keep what he has stolen. He will have to give it back!

I'm going to show you how this works. I'm going to give you the Word to prove it. Then I'm going to share with you a testimony from my own experience.

In 1 Thessalonians 1:6, we read: "And ye became followers of us, and of the Lord, having received the word in much affliction, with joy of the Holy Ghost." Notice these words: "having received the word in much affliction, with joy of the Holy Ghost." Note the progression here. *First the Word, then affliction, then joy!*

These people received the Word gladly. Then the devil came to get that Word, but his afflictions only led to joy. Satan could steal their possessions, their worldly goods, but he couldn't steal their joy—and without their joy, he couldn't keep their goods!

The apostle Paul tells us in his writings to Timothy to "fight the good fight of faith" (1 Tim. 6:12). Even though the devil may be trying his best to steal everything you have, you are still capable of fighting the fight of faith as long as you have joy. Many Christians get sidetracked because, at the first symptom of lack, they lose their joy.

To them, it's "I've got the victory" in the morning. But because of some mishap that day, it's "I lost the victory" that evening! Some people are *on the mountain* in the morning and *in the valley* by nightfall! When you find believers who are joyful whatever the circumstances may be, then you have found some winners. You can't beat a believer who is joyful.

Remember what James said: "My brethren, count it all joy when ye fall into divers temptations [testings, trials]" (James 1:2). I used to read that and think it *had* to be a misprint. God couldn't have said, *"Count it all joy* when you are tempted, tested, and tried."

I thought, *Lord, surely You didn't expect me to be full of joy when the devil blew up my car!*

He said, "No, I'm not telling you to do anything so foolish as to give thanks for the trial. I am telling you not to let anything get your joy. Son, as long as you have your joy, you're still in the game; you're still undefeated."

Now I want to share a couple of things just the way the Lord shared them with me. Satan loves to put you on trial and make a public spectacle of you because you have made a decision to stand on the Word of God. His plan is to create so much pressure around you that you will fold up and quit. Since he is a thief by nature, he will do his utmost to steal your material goods, so that you will become discouraged. But even if he has your money and your material possessions, you can still be the winner as long as you have the Word in your heart.

When these things happen, if you'll resolve in your own mind, *This situation doesn't alter the Word one bit,* and if you will stay on that Word, then the situation has to change, because the Word won't! It doesn't make any difference what happens to you, the Word never changes. As long as you have the Word in your heart, you will still have joy—and that joy will cause everything you've lost to be restored to you in full!

You can't praise God and be discouraged at the same time. You can't offer joy—the sacrifice of joy, the sacrifice of praise, the sacrifice of thanksgiving—and be discouraged simultaneously. You may be discouraged; but once you begin to offer a sacrifice of joy, it won't be a sacrifice anymore. Then it becomes an act of your will.

Satan is after your joy—and he doesn't care what evil tactic he has to use to get it. If you've never realized this before, learn now: *Satan wants your joy!* Why? Very simple. The Word produces joy. If he can get the Word out of your heart, he can stop that flow of joy. Once he gets your joy, he has you and everything you possess. If he can capture your *joy,* he has defeated *you.*

But Jesus said, "Your joy no *man* taketh from you" (John 16:22). If no man can take it, then neither can the devil—unless you allow it. Instead of giving up when Satan tries to spoil your goods and steal from you, you need to give voice to joy.

GIVE VOICE TO JOY

God has promised to do certain things for people who will not allow their joy to be stolen. Perhaps you believed God for a beautiful new car only to have it demolished a few weeks later by a drunken driver. Or you may have bought a new dress or suit for a vacation trip only to have it stolen from your hotel room.

When these things happen, what is your reaction? Do you get discouraged? Do you ask yourself why God would give you something only to turn around and take it from you? He didn't; the devil did! Satan doesn't care what he has to create in order to steal from you.

There have been several times that I had need of a certain amount of money, so I believed God for it. But as soon as I got that money, something went wrong. The refrigerator quit, the car broke down, or some other unexpected expense came up. Before I could use the money I had believed God for, some emergency expense would eat it up. I got so tired of needing money all the time! The devil was stealing from us, trying to harass and torment us and keep us on the run.

Many times such harassment will cause us to become discouraged and lose our joy. But, friend, I'm going to tell you again: *If Satan can't get your joy, he can't defeat you. Not only that, you're going to get back all that was stolen from you!*

Instead of getting discouraged and giving up, you should give voice to joy. Did you know that joy has a voice? Well, it does! Let's look at Jeremiah 33:11:

> *The voice of joy, and the voice of gladness, the voice of the bridegroom, and the voice of the bride, the voice of them that shall say, Praise the Lord of hosts: for the Lord is good; for his mercy endureth for ever: and of them that shall bring the sacrifice of praise into the house of the Lord. For I will cause to return the captivity of the land, as at the first, saith the Lord.*

The New American Standard Bible says: "For I will restore the fortunes of the land as they were at first."

Do you know what "the fortunes of the land" are? *Your possessions—your goods.* In other words, God is saying, "You took joyfully the spoiling of your goods. Now I will restore them to you in full!"

Satan had stolen from these people something that was theirs—their land, their goods, their property—yet they remained joyful. They would not let him steal their joy. Here God is saying if they will give voice to that joy and not let Satan steal it from them, He will return the captivity of their land and possessions.

As long as joy is still going forth out of our mouths, God promises to get back our stolen goods for us! That is good news!

SEVENFOLD RETURN

However, that is not the end of it. This is the part that really gets me going. God told me, "Son, if the devil can't get your joy, he can't hold on to your possessions. If he can't get your joy, he can't keep your goods. I will return them. I've even made provision in My Word to see that it comes back sevenfold."

You know, when the devil has to start paying back seven times over, he will quit stealing from you. Proverbs 6:30-31 says:

Men do not despise a thief, if he steal to satisfy his soul when he is hungry; but if he be found, he shall restore sevenfold; he shall give all the substance of his house.

God wants us in the flood stage. He wants blessings coming to us both ways—a hundredfold return on everything we give and a sevenfold return on everything the devil takes from us. I don't know about you, but to me that is cause for joy!

God says, "If *a thief be found*." If you find him (catch him stealing from you), he shall restore to you sevenfold what he has stolen and give all the substance of his house.

Well, I want you to know, I've found that rat! I know who and what he is!

I believe for the hundredfold return on my giving for the Gospel's sake. I believe for the windows of heaven to be opened to me because I am a tither. I also believe I have coming to me a sevenfold return on everything the devil has stolen from me. I began to recall all the things Satan has stolen from me; then I told him, "Devil, you are a thief and you've stolen from me. Now give it back, all of it—sevenfold!" He started getting it back to me.

The testimony I am about to share is in no way meant to boast or brag on me and my faith. It is meant as a testimony to the Word of God and to His faithfulness. It's one thing to preach; it's another thing to live what you preach and preach what you live.

Once the devil stole $3,000 from me. This is how it happened. We bought a home that was set on an acre of land. It had been an old estate, and there were over thirty trees on it. Carolyn had always wanted this old house so she could restore it. Finally we sold the new home we had built and bought this beautiful old place.

It had been lovely at one time. There was a fish pond, fountains, and extensive grounds. When new, it had been beautifully landscaped, but it had not been taken care of. To get it back into shape would be quite a job.

The trees and shrubs had not been cared for in a long while. Then we discovered that the trees were dying. Since the trees were one of the main reasons we had bought the place, we called a man to come out and see what was causing the problem.

The man looked them over and told Carolyn that five different kinds of insects were eating them up. When asked for an estimate on the cost, he figured it up and said it would be about $500. So Carolyn okayed the job.

When he had finished treating the trees, he said, "You really need to have these trees trimmed. They haven't been taken care of in a long time."

When she asked him how much this would cost, he told her the whole job would probably be around $5,000. When she came to me about it later, I said, "There are other things we need to do besides spending $5,000 on trees." We were restoring the entire house, replacing the carpets, drapes, etc., and I couldn't see spending that kind of money on trees. Besides, we really didn't have the extra money.

We told the man no, but that maybe we would check with him about it later. So he left.

After that, Carolyn and I took the girls and went to Florida for a meeting. When we came home and drove up to the house, there were trucks parked in front. The next day when I came home from the office, men were in the trees with a machine that was chewing up all of those huge tree limbs. The man we had talked to was standing there with a clipboard in his hand, supervising the operation.

I walked over to him and said, "What are you doing?"

"Trimming your trees."

"Who told you to trim my trees?"

"I thought you wanted them trimmed."

I said, "I told you I didn't want them trimmed, at least not now."

"Well, I thought you did."

"No, I didn't give you permission to do it. We signed a contract on the first job, but not on this. Get those men out of my trees."

He said, "I've already completed $3,000 worth of work. You owe me that much."

"No, I don't! I didn't give you permission to do this job, and you know it." I could tell that in just a little bit I was going to lose my joy. (I had a strong urge to sin then get forgiveness later!)

My first reaction was, *I'm not paying $3,000. I'll just talk to my attorney.* I knew my attorney would tell me not to pay. If I took him to court, I would win because there was no contract. I had the guy dead to rights, and I knew it.

But then a Scripture came up inside me: "Walk in love" (Eph. 5:2). Next, I heard this question: "What would Jesus do?" Immediately, I could see Jesus with a whip in His hand, running the moneychangers out of the temple

(John 2:15). I thought, *Where's my whip?* I was ready to beat this guy.

"No," the Holy Spirit said, "that's a different situation."

"But, Lord," I said, "why do I have to walk in love when I didn't start this? Tell him to walk in love."

The Lord answered, "He doesn't know anything about love."

"Then please explain to me, Lord, exactly what You mean by walking in love in this situation."

"Pay the man."

"But, Lord, I don't have the extra $3,000 to pay this."

"I didn't say anything about extra. I said to pay him."

"But, Lord, I have that money set aside for something else."

"Pay him. Love never fails. I'll get it back to you."

To be honest with you, I didn't want to do it. I wanted to fight. But I went into the house and talked to Carolyn about it. "What are we going to do, Carolyn?"

"Well, God is telling me to walk in love."

"You too, huh? Okay, where's the checkbook?"

You can tell by my attitude that there was very little love in what I was doing. Sometimes, you know, we have to walk in love *by faith.*

I was complaining while I wrote the check. Then the Lord asked me, "You *do* want this back, don't you?"

"I sure do."

"Then you'd better change your attitude."

So I swallowed hard. Then Carolyn and I joined hands and prayed: "Father, in the name of Jesus, we're going to walk in love in this situation. We're going to give the man the $3,000."

Then the Lord reminded me that the thief has to repay sevenfold. He said, "Satan stole that money from you, but love never fails. Don't let this steal your joy. Right now, I want you to lay hold on the sevenfold return."

So with joy, I gave the man my check for $3,000.

Later as I was driving to the office, I told the devil, "You're going to give back that money sevenfold, in the name of Jesus!"

As time went by, I would think about it occasionally and say, "Satan, you're going to pay back that money sevenfold." But gradually I just forgot about it.

Then one morning the Lord revealed to me this Scripture about taking joyfully the spoiling of our goods. Suddenly I remembered that incident. I said, "Devil, you remember that $3,000 you stole from me on those trees?

In the name of Jesus, I demand that you get it back to me sevenfold! You're not stealing my joy and you can't keep my goods!"

A few days later as I was relaxing at home, the telephone rang. It was a man I had met a couple of weeks before. He said, "God spoke to my wife and me last week and told us to do something. I've flown here to Fort Worth to obey the Lord. If possible, I'd like for you to have breakfast with me in the morning so I can talk with you."

The next morning I met him at the airport for breakfast. While we were talking and fellowshipping, he said, "God spoke to me about $3,000 the devil stole from you. My wife and I have been instructed of the Lord to give it back to you sevenfold."

Then he reached into his pocket and handed me an envelope. It contained $21,000 in cash! Now most of the money given to us goes into the ministry, and we are paid a salary just like everybody else. But this man said, "This doesn't go to your ministry. God dealt with us about giving it to you and your wife personally. The devil stole $3,000 from you personally, and this is that money returned to you seven times over. Use it any way you want." Then he casually commented, "You might want to put it on your house." That was exactly what we were believing God for.

Since then, Carolyn and I have been working on the devil to give back all he has stolen from us—and he has been bringing it in sevenfold!

If Satan can't steal your joy, he can't keep your goods. Do you believe that? If you do, it's time to take your stand and get back your goods. The devil has tried his best to steal your finances, your material possessions, and your joy. But if you have the spiritual audacity to stand on the authority of God's Word and not let him get your joy, he can't rob you. No matter what he tries to steal, don't let him get your joy. Even if he does get your finances or any of your material possessions, it's only temporary; he can't keep them if he can't get your joy.

With this bit of information there is no reason for a Christian to ever get down. When Satan comes against a child of God, all he does is create more trouble for himself. God has made provision for us both ways. We give—and there's a return on it. Satan steals from us—and there's a return on that, too!

Think for a moment of all the things Satan has stolen from you since you have been a Christian. Start now to expose him and his thievery. Rebuke him in the name of Jesus Christ. On the authority of God's Word, order him to return sevenfold everything he has unlawfully taken from you. You have that right!

HOW TO PRAY

Pray this prayer right now out loud:

Heavenly Father, by the authority of Your Word, You said that whatever I bind on earth is bound in heaven and whatever I loose on earth is loosed in heaven.

Satan, I bind you. I bind the principalities and the powers. I bind every demon spirit that has been assigned against me and my family to steal from us, to rob us of our goods and of our joy. I bind you, evil spirits, and I bind you, thief, in the name of Jesus Christ of Nazareth.

Satan, you are a thief and you've been found. In the name of Jesus, I command you to return to me sevenfold everything you've stolen from me. I loose all my goods, in Jesus' name, to come back to me sevenfold according to God's Word.

Thank You, Father, for restoring to me seven times over all that is rightfully mine. I receive it, Lord. I thank You and praise You for it, in the name of Jesus Christ. Amen.

2

...HE CAN'T DEFEAT YOU

Jesus has told us that joy is a product of the spoken Word. In the fourth chapter of Mark, He said that once the Word is sown in a man's heart, Satan comes *immediately* to take it away.

The New American Standard Bible translates Matthew's version of this statement this way: "the evil one comes and *snatches away* what has been sown in his heart" (Matt. 13:19). Why? Because the Word of God produces joy in the heart.

As long as you have the Word in your heart, you will have joy in your heart. Then no matter what the devil does, he can't totally defeat you.

The devil knows that the most advantageous time to try to steal the Word from you is right after you've received it. He knows better than to wait until you've spent time in meditation and fellowship with God so that the Word has become deeply rooted in your heart and has become a revelation to you.

THE WORD IS VITAL

Philippians 4:19 is as real to me as my own right arm—and as useful. It became a part of me many years ago when it looked as if there was no way I would get my needs met. But I began confessing that verse: "My God supplies all my need according to His riches in glory by Christ Jesus."

At times, I would wake up at night in a cold sweat with the devil saying, "You're going to fail. You're going to lose everything you own. There's no way you can overcome."

I would jump out of bed and start walking the floor, saying over and over again: "My God supplies all my need according to His riches in glory by Christ Jesus." Sometimes the pressure would be so strong I wanted to shout, so I would go out into the yard and scream: "My God supplies all my need according to His riches in glory by Christ Jesus!"

Then one day I no longer had to say that Scripture to convince myself it was so. It suddenly dropped down into my heart and stuck there! Once I had taken hold of that truth, you couldn't have pried it out of me with a crowbar!

Whenever a need arose, I would say with confidence and faith: "My God supplies my every need. My God supplies my every need." And He did!

BE OF GOOD CHEER

Obviously it is to Satan's advantage to attack when you first hear the Word and try to snatch it away through some kind of adversity. That's his plan. If he can create enough pressure and adversity, you will be tempted to fall prey to that adversity and become discouraged.

Many times in the Old Testament God told His people, "Be of good courage. Be not dismayed. Fear not." The phrase, "Be of good courage," isn't used often in the New Testament. Jesus said it this way: "Be of good cheer."

In John 16:33, Jesus said, "In the world ye shall have tribulation." Some people stop reading here and think we are supposed to have tribulation all the time. But Jesus hadn't finished talking. He said, "In the world ye shall have tribulation: but be of good cheer; I have overcome the world" (John 16:33). Don't read, "In the world ye shall have tribulation," and then close the book. If you do, you'll identify with the wrong part of the verse—the tribulation and adversity.

Psalm 34:19 says, "Many are the afflictions of the righteous." People stop reading there and say, "Yes, many are the afflictions of the righteous; and, dear God, I'm afflicted!" But the psalmist didn't stop there. He said, "Many are the afflictions of the righteous: but the Lord delivereth him out of them all" (Ps. 34:19). This is what the psalmist actually said. It paints a different picture, doesn't it?

When reading portions of Scripture, you should read the entire context to avoid identifying with the wrong thing. Jesus said, "Be of good cheer; I have overcome the world." That's the part we should identify with. *Be of good cheer!*

Why do we have cheerleaders in our schools? To provoke the people, to generate enthusiasm, to inject life and energy into the players.

Suppose cheerleaders led a cheer like this: "Give me a D! Give me an E! Give me an F! Give me an E! Give me an A! Give me a T! What's that spell? *DEFEAT!*"

That's not a good cheer. Our cheerleaders don't do that. They yell out: Give me a V! Give me an I! Give me a C! Give me a T! Give me an O! Give me an R! Give me a

Y! What's that spell? *VICTORY!*" That kind of cheer will get the fans and players excited.

Well, I've found out that I can cheer myself on. Sometimes when the devil tries to inject me with discouragement and rob me of my joy, I'll lead myself in a cheer: "Jerry, get ready! Give me a J! Give me an E! Give me an S! Give me a U! Give me an S! What's that spell? *JESUS!* What does that mean? *Victory!*" If someone were to hear me, they might think I was nuts, but I'm not nuts—I'm of good cheer!

Satan is out to get your joy. If he can get it, he will totally defeat you. He'll create situations so he can spoil your goods and snatch them away. But, as we have seen, as long as he can't get your joy, he can't keep your goods, and he can't defeat you. So be of good cheer!

PRAISING GOD FOR DELIVERANCE

Let's look at Hebrews 10:32-34 again, this time in the New American Standard Bible:

But remember the former days, when, after being enlightened, you endured a great conflict of sufferings, partly by being made a public spectacle through reproaches and tribulations, and partly by becoming sharers with those who were so treated. For you showed sympathy [or compassion] *to the prisoners and accepted joyfully the seizure of your property.*

The King James Version says, "For ye...took joyfully the spoiling of your goods" (v. 34). Notice again that Satan had come in and spoiled these people's goods. But this says their attitude was not one of sorrow or depression, but rather of joy.

Now that doesn't mean they said, "Praise the Lord, the devil just stole our car. Praise the Lord, I've got cancer." No!

A few years ago a certain teaching became popular. Some folks were preaching that Christians ought to praise God for every bad thing that happens because "this is the will of God concerning you." That's not what God said. In 1 Thessalonians 5:16-18, He does say:

Rejoice evermore. Pray without ceasing. In every thing give thanks: for this is the will of God in Christ Jesus concerning you.

This doesn't say to praise God for evil things. God isn't the evil doer. Why should we thank God for something which doesn't come from Him?

People would say things like, "Praise God that you have cancer because that's His will. Praise God because your husband is an alcoholic and your children are on drugs because praise stops the avenger."

Praise *does* stop the avenger, but God didn't tell us to praise Him for problems. He said to give thanks *"in* everything," not *"for* everything." We should praise God in the midst of our problems. But we're not praising Him for the problem; we're praising Him for deliverance from the problem! He isn't the god of the *problem;* He's the God of deliverance.

Whenever you praise God for a problem, the "god" of the problem—Satan—is getting your praise. If you say, "I just praise God for my cancer," the god of cancer gets the praise. That means Satan is finally in the position he has been trying to attain since iniquity was found in him. He has always sought to exalt himself above the most High God. He wants praise. He wants the praise of God's people. The only way he can get it is to deceive them into thinking God is the one who is giving them heart trouble, cancer, and all the other diabolical things that have been authored by the devil.

No, God isn't saying, "Praise Me *for* adversity." He is saying, "Praise Me *in* all things, in every kind of situation. Don't let the devil get your joy. If you will praise Me in all things, I'll deliver you from them and see that you are set free because praise stops the avenger."

NO MAN CAN TAKE YOUR JOY

Satan is a thief. When he creates attacks against you, it is to steal something from you. His ultimate motive is to get the joy in your heart. But Jesus said, "Your joy *no man taketh from* you" (John 16:22). I want to add something to that. The Scriptures will bear me out. If man can't take your joy, neither can the devil—not unless you allow it.

No one can take your joy from you. No matter how bad things get, if you will continue to rejoice, your joy cannot be taken away. The only way you can lose it is by an act of your will. You have to willfully give it up.

This is very important. The devil can't take your joy from you, but he can create enough pressure around you until you willfully give it up. If you fall for his deception and give up your joy, then he has totally defeated you. Without joy, which comes from the Word of God, you have no foundation on which to stand. You become open game for the enemy.

Always remember this: Satan may come against you, but he can't defeat you unless you let him. He may try to take your car, your finances, or the life of a loved one, but until he gets your joy, he can't defeat you. As long as you're still praising God and still have a joyful heart, the game isn't over.

We have already seen that if Satan can't get your joy, he can't keep what he has stolen from you. We also saw in Proverbs 6:30-31 that if a thief is found out, he must restore sevenfold. We have the right to claim a sevenfold return on anything the devil steals from us.

Then Jeremiah 33:11 taught us about the *voice of joy,* that to those who *shall bring the sacrifice of praise,* God has promised to *cause to return the captivity of the land.* God has promised that regardless of what adversity we encounter, He will cause to be returned to us everything that has been wrongfully taken by the enemy—*if* we will not lose our joy but continue to praise Him.

That is good news! I have made a quality decision that I will not let anything rob me of my joy. I have ample opportunity to fail daily. Each glorious new dawn brings new opportunity to fold up and quit. But, thank God, I'm not going to quit, regardless of what the day may bring. I refuse to let anything get my joy. As long as I have joy, it doesn't make any difference what Satan does he can't defeat me. I'm still in the game.

Not only does each new day bring new opportunity to fail, it also brings new opportunity to succeed! Each new day brings another turn at bat. I'm friends with the Umpire. The Umpire is the Judge of all the earth, and He will do what is right. He is God.

As Kenneth Copeland says, "Don't play nine-inning ball games; play until you win."

Stay in the game until you emerge victorious, no matter how long that may take. If Satan gives you any lip about it, take the sword of the Spirit as a bat and bust him in the head. Your Father will support you—He's the Umpire.

The best part is that the devil doesn't get a turn at bat! Jesus pitched a no-hitter against that rat many years ago. He took the bat away from him, busted him in the head with it, and threw him out of the game. He took the enemy's armor, stripped him of his authority, took the keys of death, hell, and the grave, and triumphed over him completely!

That was the last time Satan got to bat. Since then the only time he can bat is when he deceives you into letting him take your turn. If you're like most Christians, you have been throwing the ball to him year after year and letting him beat you all over the park.

Some people complain about how rough "the game of life" is. They drop their heads and moan that they don't have a chance in life, that they already have "two strikes against them."

Friend, it doesn't matter if there are *three* strikes against you, you're not out! The Umpire is your Father, and He makes the rules of this game. You can stay at bat until you hit the ball! How can you lose in a game like that?

OVERCOME EVIL WITH GOOD

You know, sometimes it is difficult to stand your ground and make the opponent play the game the way you want it played. But it can be done. It just takes determination, an all-out commitment on your part.

I remember one time I made a decision, and it turned out to be one of the hardest decisions I've ever had to back up. You know, when you make a decision to do something, you get an opportunity to act on it. Have you ever decided that you were going to take control over your mouth, that you were only going to use it to bless others? Then some unlovely Christian crossed your path. You got an opportunity right away to back up that commitment, didn't you?

I once made a decision that I wasn't going to retaliate when evil was done to me, that I wasn't going to repay evil with evil. The Bible says, "Be not overcome of evil, but overcome evil with good" (Rom. 12:21). I decided that when people did me wrong, I would not retaliate by doing them wrong—that, come what may, I was going to walk in love. Well, before nightfall I had an opportunity to back up my decision. That was one of the hardest decisions I have ever had to stand by.

The devil doesn't know how to handle a person who keeps rejoicing in the face of destruction.

Let me give you an example. Take the apostle Paul. In 2 Corinthians 12:7, he said that a messenger of Satan had been sent to buffet him. In chapter 11, he listed many things the devil had tried to do to keep him from preaching the Gospel: shipwreck, stonings, beatings, perils of robbers, perils in his journeys, perils of his own countrymen, weariness, painfulness, hunger, thirst, cold, nakedness (2 Corinthians 11:25-27). He talked about every hard thing the devil had thrown at him to try to make him give up and quit.

These were no lightweight things the apostle Paul endured—stonings, shipwreck, being left for dead, beatings, imprisonment. He suffered all these things for the Gospel's sake. Paul had to contend with more than just a headache and a runny nose! The devil was out to destroy him. Then in 2 Corinthians 4:17, Paul had the audacity to refer to all these things as "our light affliction"!

Don't you know it was hard on the devil, after firing his best shots, to hear Paul shrug them off and report to the Corinthians that he had met the enemy and had only encountered "light resistance"? It's hard on Satan when he thinks he has maneuvered and manipulated things, creating pressure and adversity to wipe you out, and you keep rejoicing. He doesn't know how to handle that.

THE POWER OF PRAISE

Do you remember what the leaders of God's people in the Old Testament did when outnumbered by the enemy? Many times the man in charge would seek God and call a solemn fast. All the people would then seek God for guidance, and He would deliver them despite the seeming hopelessness of their situation.

King Jehoshaphat did this once (2 Chron. 20:14-25). He called a solemn fast when Judah was surrounded by a huge army that outnumbered them and threatened to destroy them. The people fasted, prayed, and sought God about how to handle the situation. The Spirit of God moved upon one of the men in the congregation, and he began to speak. Through him the Lord instructed Jehoshaphat, "Send your singers out ahead of the army. Have them shout with a loud voice, *Praise the Lord; for his mercy endureth for ever*" (2 Chron. 20:21).

God didn't choose His skilled swordsmen, the mighty men of battle, to lead His forces. He chose the praisers and put them out on the front line. Those people began to march out against the enemy who outnumbered them. As they walked to face the enemy, they began to sing and shout, to lift their voices in one accord: "Praise the Lord! For His mercy endures forever! Praise ye the Lord!"

Now that has to be hard on the enemy who knows he outnumbers Judah and assumes they are afraid and shaking in their boots; then all of a sudden they come marching against him with head held high, shouting praises to God. That enemy didn't know how to react to this unexpected show of force and spirit. In their confusion they actually turned on each other and began to fight and kill their own men. Then God's people just walked in and gathered up the spoil that was left after the enemy had routed itself. There was so much spoil that it took three days to gather up all of it (2 Chron. 20:25).

You can't defeat praisers. You can't defeat one who is quick to praise God.

Do you know what the word *Judah* means? It means "praise." Jesus came from the tribe of Judah. We're joint-heirs with Jesus, so that means we are also of the tribe of Judah. We are praisers, and a praiser can't be defeated.

God has told us through the apostle Paul, "Rejoice in the Lord alway: and again I say, Rejoice" (Phil. 4:4). He also said, "The joy of the Lord is your strength" (Neh. 8:10). In 1 Thessalonians 5:18, He tells us, "In every thing give thanks." The psalmist writes: "O clap your hands, all ye people; shout unto God with the voice of triumph" (Ps. 47:1); "Rejoice in the Lord, O ye righteous" (Ps. 33:1); "Praise ye the Lord" (Ps. 146:1; 147:1; 148:1; 149:1; 150:1).

The Bible doesn't tell us all these things about rejoicing, giving thanks, and praising God for nothing. *There is strength in praise! There is strength in rejoicing! There is strength in thanksgiving!* The devil doesn't know what to do when he has launched an attack against you, and you keep praising the Lord.

THE POWER OF LAUGHTER

God says that joy has a voice. One of the ways you can release joy is through laughter.

You know, many of God's people don't know how to laugh. One of the things that kept me out of Christianity for so long was Christians—those long-faced, poor-me, sad sacks who called themselves "children of light" and went around looking like death. They were trying to convince me to be like them, but I didn't want any part of something that made you look like that!

Christians need to learn how to laugh. In the past we've had the mistaken idea that to be a Christian you were supposed to be so "holy and spiritual" that you never smiled.

Since I became a Christian, I've never had so much fun in my life! I never had this much fun and enjoyment in life before I became a believer. I have found more to laugh about since I came to God than I ever did when I was still under bondage to Satan. Who do you think is happier, livelier, and more joyously cheerful: the slave or the free man?

As a kid growing up, it was my nature to be humorous. I enjoyed making people laugh. There was just a funny side to me, and I always had the ability to come up with something funny at a moment when something funny needed to be said. One of the reasons I didn't want to go into the ministry was all of the preachers I saw. They looked like the last time they had had any fun was the day before they got born again.

I thought, *Dear Lord, You mean to tell me if I become a Christian, if I become a minister, that everything has to be solemn and serious? Will I have to go around with a long face and never have any joy or fun anymore?* That didn't appeal to me at all.

But in the Bible it talked about joy, rejoicing, and laughter. It talked about being of good cheer. My Bible told me not to fear or be dismayed or have worried thoughts about anything. Jesus said, "Take no thought for your life" (Matt. 6:25). It seemed to me that Christianity in its highest form would be the happiest life anyone could ever live.

That's one thing that caused me to identify so much with Brother Copeland. When I heard him that first night, he said some things that were hilarious. He made the Word come alive. That funny side allowed him to say things in a way that would amuse while they enlightened. When I met Kenneth Copeland, I discovered to my delight that you can be a Christian, even a minister of the Gospel, and still have a sense of humor.

You can't be burdened down with problems and have joy and laughter at the same time.

You ought to learn to laugh, if for no other reason than just to keep the pressure off of you. Look at Job 5:22: "At destruction and famine thou shalt laugh." Laugh! At destruction and famine thou shalt *laugh*.

Somebody might say, "Now, brother, I just don't believe we're to laugh at famine and destruction. We need to take it more seriously than that." I didn't write this verse; God did! And God is talking to Job. If anybody ever had famine and destruction, it was Job. If anybody had a reason not to laugh, it was Job. In the natural realm, he had problems! But we're not dealing with the natural, we're dealing with the supernatural. God told Job, "At famine and destruction thou shalt laugh." Do you know why? He was trying to get the man into a position where he wouldn't lose his joy.

It was God who made Job wealthy in the first place. But Job destroyed it because of his fear. He said, "The thing which I greatly feared is come upon me, and that which I was afraid of is come unto me" (Job 3:25). It wasn't God who did those things to Job. Job got himself into trouble with his big mouth. Finally in chapter 6, Job makes this statement: "Teach me, and I will hold my tongue" (v. 24). Then he says, "How forcible are right words!" (v. 25). Job finally realized that it was his mouth that had gotten him into trouble. He had been talking in fear, and that which he so greatly feared came upon him. But God told him that one of the ways to get delivered of this situation was laughter. "At famine and destruction thou shalt laugh."

God isn't telling us to pretend that problems don't exist. He is telling us to refuse to let the devil steal our joy. Don't let him steal your joy. "At famine and destruction thou shalt laugh." Why? Because laughter releases joy, and *joy is a spiritual force.*

Joy can put your enemy in such turmoil that he doesn't know how to handle you. I'm convinced that it's the same way in the ranks of Satan as it was in those enemy forces who came against Judah in King Jehoshaphat's day. When God's people began to praise the Lord, their enemies were so confounded that they turned on one another.

I am convinced that there is confusion in Satan's camp when he comes against a child of God who will not let his joy be taken out of his heart but who continues to worship, praise, and rejoice in God. If you will laugh at the enemy and rejoice in the fact that God is able to deliver you, the enemy can't prevail against you. *Satan's forces don't know how to handle praise and rejoicing.*

In the natural, the obvious thing to do is to tuck our heads and accept defeat. Our natural human reaction is to just fold our hands and find a good place to cry. Satan really likes for you to get into a pity party: "Poor old me, nobody cares about me. My husband doesn't care. My kids don't care. Nobody cares."

In the first place that's a lie—God cares. It is easy to get into a pity party. But while you are in that pity party, you are losing your joy. "At famine and destruction thou shalt laugh." *Laughter is the way to release joy.*

YET WILL I REJOICE

Although the fig tree shall not blossom, neither shall fruit be in the vines; the labour of the olive shall fail, and the fields shall yield no meat; the flock shall be cut off from the fold, and there shall be no herd in the stalls.

Habakkuk 3:17

Mr. Habakkuk has some problems here. He can't get his figs to grow. He can't get any fruit on the vine. His olives are failing. His fields are not producing. His flocks have been cut off from the fold. His cattle are missing from the stalls. Despite the calamities that have befallen him, look what he says in the next verse:

Yet I will rejoice in the Lord, I will joy in the God of my salvation.

Habakkuk 3:18

Now here is a fellow the devil can't beat. Satan has come against him by every available avenue, but the guy still comes up praising God. You can't beat a man like that.

"I will joy in the God of my salvation." Do you know what salvation is? Deliverance. The reason Habakkuk could continue to rejoice, even in the midst of adversity, was that he had an inside tip. He knew the game wasn't over just because of the way things looked at the moment. He looked beyond the circumstances to the God of his salvation. He didn't see himself *defeated;* he saw himself *delivered!*

The Lord God is my strength, and he will make my feet like hinds' feet, and he will make me to walk upon mine high places.

Habakkuk 3:19

Habakkuk said, "I'm not discouraged by all of this. I know how it's going to turn out. I'm going to get hinds' feet. God is going to cause me to jump right over this problem!"

I like what the psalmist said: "For by thee I have run through a troop; and by my God have I leaped over a wall" (Ps. 18:29).

When the devil has lined up all of his forces and you are outnumbered, when it looks as though you are surrounded by walls on all sides and there seems to be no way of escape, God can make your feet like hinds' feet so that you too can "run through a troop" and "leap over a wall." As long as you refuse to allow the devil to steal your joy, you aren't out of the game yet. God will deliver you.

Can you look adversity straight in the eye and still rejoice? By nature, man isn't accustomed to doing such a thing. But as Christians we are supposed to overcome adversity through rejoicing. The sad fact is that most Christians don't know this.

Someone has said, "Well, that will take some doing on my part. Dear God, I've been taught all my life that when you've got problems, cry!"

Yes, it will take some discipline. It's going to mean jerking yourself up out of that bed of despondency and self-pity where you've been lying for so long. It's going to mean an end to weeping and wailing and excuse-making. No more lying down and accepting defeat.

You're going to have to pull yourself up by the ear sometimes. I've had to do that, literally. I've grabbed myself by the ear, jerked myself up out of that bed, stood myself in front of a mirror, pointed my finger at myself, and said: "Jerry Savelle, in the name of Jesus Christ, quit acting like this. You're a child of God! What are you doing lying over there as though God has fallen off His throne, as though the name of Jesus has lost its power, as though the Word of God is no longer vital and strong and powerful! What's wrong with you, boy? Get up! The Word of God has been spoken, and the Word says you win! Start talking the Word of God! Start rejoicing!"

Somebody may say, "This guy is nuts! He talks to himself in the mirror!"

Well, why not? The person who thinks I'm nuts for doing cheers in front of my mirror is the very one who does the same thing in reverse. He looks in the mirror and tells himself: "You're so mistreated. Nobody loves you. You work your fingers to the bone for people, and they don't even care. Nobody ever appreciates you. You may as well quit because nobody cares whether you make it or not."

Why shouldn't I cheer? It's scriptural! Paul said, "Rejoice evermore" (1 Thess. 5:16). Jesus told us, "Be of good cheer" (John 16:33). David encouraged us, "Be glad in the Lord, and rejoice" (Ps. 32:11).

But besides being scriptural, it's good for us. Solomon, the wisest man who ever lived, said, "A merry heart doeth good like a medicine" (Prov. 17:22). Christians need a good dose of merriment every day. I've met some Christians who look like they need to overdose on joy every morning before breakfast!

Habakkuk said, "Even in the midst of all this adversity, yet will I rejoice" (Hab. 3:1-18). Satan couldn't get that man's joy. And, my friend, I'll say it again: *If the devil can't get your joy, he can't defeat you.* You can't be defeated if you keep your joy.

GOD LAUGHS

Did you know that God laughs? If He can talk, surely He can laugh. Anybody who can talk can laugh.

The first time I found this out, I didn't know it was in the Bible. I discovered that God laughs because *I heard him laughing.* You see, I know the voice of God. I recognize it when I hear it.

One time I found myself in a situation in which it looked as though I was bound to fail. There seemed to be no way out. So I went into my study, sat down at my desk, and laid my Bible out. I said, "Now, Father, here's the problem. Here's what man says; here's what the devil says; and here's what Your Word says."

Then I started reading the Word. Suddenly inside me—in the same place I hear His voice speaking—I heard laughter. It surprised me, and I thought, *That's not me.*

I said, "Lord, is that You laughing?"

He said, "Yes."

I said, "What are You laughing at?" Then I got tickled listening to Him. I was laughing because God was laughing. I could hear Him laughing inside me. Finally, when I managed to get my breath, I said, "Lord, what are we laughing at?"

"The devil. He thinks he's going to win."

"But, Lord, it does look that way."

"Yes. That's what's so funny." Then He started laughing again.

Your obvious question at this point would be: "Is this scriptural?"

Let's look at Psalm 2:

Why are the nations in an uproar and the peoples devising a vain thing? The kings of the earth take their stand, and the rulers take counsel together against the Lord and against His Anointed, saying, "Let us tear their fetters apart, and cast away their cords from us!" He who sits in the heavens laughs, the Lord scoffs at them.

Psalm 2:1-4 NASB

"He who sits in the heavens laughs." Well, who is sitting in the heavens? God. To see what He is laughing at, let's look in Psalm 37:

> *The wicked plots against the righteous, and gnashes at him with his teeth. The Lord laughs at him, for He sees his day is coming.*
>
> Psalm 37:12-13 NASB

This is what the Lord was laughing at: the devil's plots and schemes. Satan is so obvious to God that he is laughable.

LAUGHING AT SATAN

The Lord told me, "That's what I'm laughing at, Son. The devil is trying to prove to you that you are going to fail and he is going to win. I'm laughing because his day is coming."

Then He said, "What I want you to do is rejoice. I want you to give voice to joy. As My Word says, 'At [the signs of] destruction and famine thou shalt laugh' (Job 5:22).

I started laughing again, but this time I wasn't just laughing because God was laughing. I was laughing because I had gotten hold of a truth.

It is hard for you to rejoice if you don't know what the Word says. In fact, that's the reason it would be difficult for me to try to provoke you to rejoice through this book. If you don't know what the Word of God says about your situation, you won't be able to rejoice. I might get you to smile, chuckle, or even laugh because of something humorous I might write. I might manage to amuse you for a while in these pages, but I can't move you to sincerely rejoice unless you know what God's Word says about you and about your enemy, Satan.

But once you know who you are in Christ, once you realize your authority as a believer and the significance of your inheritance as a saint, there is real cause for rejoicing. For you to truly rejoice, you must know where you stand with God. You must know that God is on your side in this situation, and if God be for you, who could dare be against you (Rom. 8:31)? When you get full of the Word of God, Satan and his dirty little tricks become a laughing matter.

Laughter is a powerful force against the wiles of the enemy. Satan doesn't know how to handle a person who takes his abuse and laughs it off.

Friend, learn to rejoice, learn to give voice to joy, learn to laugh. There is no greater possession on earth than a joyful heart. Remember, it *doeth good like a medicine.*

GOD MEETS YOU WHEN YOU REJOICE

The last Scripture I want to share with you in this chapter is found in Isaiah 64: "Thou meetest him that rejoiceth" (v. 5).

God will meet you when you rejoice. God will get in the boat with you. He will meet you in your problems, in your adversities, in your afflictions, in your troubles. If you will rejoice, God promises to meet you; and when God comes on the scene, what happens to problems? They depart!

The psalmist said of God, "In thy presence is fulness of joy" (Ps. 16:11). We need to learn to bring God into our presence when we are in the midst of trouble, because the Bible says that wherever He is, there is fullness of joy. When you have fullness of joy, there is no way the devil can defeat you.

God says that He sits in heaven laughing at His enemy because He knows his day is coming. He tells us, "At destruction and famine thou shalt laugh" (Job 5:22). Even in the midst of all adversity, Habakkuk said, "Yet I will rejoice in the Lord, I will joy in the God of my salvation" (Hab. 3:18).

Isaiah tells us that God will meet those who rejoice. God is telling us in these verses that if we will give voice to joy, even in the midst of adversity, He will meet us. He promises that no weapon formed against us will prosper. He promises to return out of captivity that which our adversary has stolen from us. Not only that, He tells us that a joyful heart is good medicine. It will heal and soothe and comfort. It will bring peace and happiness, and will cause recovery.

God is inviting you to join Him in laughter at your adversary. God wants to meet you in your rejoicing. When you do this, you will gain a new closeness with God. When you get together and have a good laugh on the devil, the situation won't look as dark as before. Your situation won't look so bleak, so terrible. It won't look as though defeat is inevitable. You will love staying in God's presence because in His presence is fullness of joy.

I like being around people who are joyful, particularly when I've had an opportunity to be down. I like to be with a person who has the ability to cheer me up. Well, God is that way. When I've had an opportunity to be down, I run to God and let Him tell me what the Word says. It's always something good, something cheering. He'll throw His arms around me and say, "What's the matter, little buddy? Why are you looking so bleak? What's the problem?"

I say, "The devil has told me I'm going to lose."

He will say, "You don't believe what the devil says, do you?"

"Well, it sure looks like I'm going to lose."

"Since when did you start living by what it looks like? I thought you walked by faith and not by sight."

"I do, but You don't understand my problem."

"Hey, wait a minute. It couldn't be bigger than Me. I'm God. Your problem couldn't possibly be bigger than Me. Have you forgotten that I'm on your side?"

"Yes, I know You're on my side, but what are we going to do about this problem?"

"Didn't I tell you that no weapon formed against you shall prosper?"

"Yes, Sir."

"Didn't I tell you that your faith will overcome the world?"

"Yes, Sir."

"Didn't I tell you that you can do all things through Christ who strengthens you?"

"Yes, Sir."

"Well then, what are we going to do about this problem?"

"What problem, Lord?"

Hang around God for a while and He'll get you out of the dumps. God doesn't stay in the dumps.

Not once have I gone into the throne room depressed and said, "God, I've been in the valley," and heard Him say, "Me, too!"

Not once will you walk into God's throne room and say, "Lord, I'm really down," and hear Him say, "Yes, I know what you mean. I feel lower than the hair on a snake's belly!"

You will never walk into God's presence and say, "God, I'm telling You, inflation's terrible. I can't even afford hamburger meat anymore," then hear Him say, "You think you have troubles. I had to lay Jesus off this morning. The angels are out on strike. I had to hock the pearly gates to pay the note on the throne room. I totaled out my chariot today, and a tornado hit the mansions on the south end. Things are just terrible up here!"

God is in charge of heaven, and things just don't go that way in heaven. Well, I have news for you, brother: God is in charge down here, too—and things are not going to go that way here for very long, not as long as you hold on to your joy!

The Bible says, "We have not an high priest which cannot be touched with the feeling of our infirmities" (Heb. 4:15). Jesus has lived on this planet. He knows what it's like here. He knows the pressures, the turmoil, the adversity. He has been confronted by the same devil who opposes you and me. He is a merciful and compassionate High Priest, who can be touched with the feeling of our infirmities. That High Priest says to come boldly to the throne and obtain mercy and find grace to help in time of need (Heb. 4:16).

When you are down, that's when you ought to run to the throne of God. Don't run *from* God—run *to* Him! God isn't going to identify with you when you are in the "mulleygrubs." But He will get you out of the "mulleygrubs" (or whatever kind of "grubs" you're in), if you'll let Him. He'll cheer you up!

The Bible says in Ephesians 1:19 that in the ages to come God is going to show *"what is the exceeding greatness of his power to us-ward who believe."* That means God is going to do everything in His power to turn you on!

My friend, I don't care how bleak your problem looks or how bad your circumstances are, if you can read your Bible, you can rejoice. And if you can rejoice, you are a candidate for victory. Right now while you are reading these words, if you can't bring yourself to laugh out loud at the devil, in the face of adversity, that's a good indication you need to learn to laugh—to laugh at destruction, to laugh at famine.

God said to rejoice and He will meet you. When God comes on the scene, there is fullness of joy; the avenger is stopped and stilled. If you don't get anything else out of this book, get this: *The devil can't defeat a joyful believer.*

The next time adversity comes your way, I challenge you to rejoice in the very midst of it. Then write and share with me what happens. Somebody might say, "Well, I tried it, and nothing happened; it got worse." Well, if that is your testimony, either you or God is lying. (And if I have to pick one—you're it!) God said He would turn the captivity. Stand on that Word of promise and you won't fail—because God won't fail.

Whatever your situation, begin to rejoice right now and praise God for the victory that is yours in Christ Jesus. Hold fast to that victory. Hold fast to your joy because *if Satan can't steal your joy, he can't defeat you!*

3

...HE CAN'T DECEIVE YOU

Hear then the parable of the sower. When anyone hears the word of the kingdom and does not understand it, the evil one comes and snatches away what has been sown in his heart. This is the one on whom seed was sown beside the road. The one on whom seed was sown on the rocky places, this is the man who hears the word and immediately receives it with joy; yet he has no firm root in himself, but is only temporary, and when affliction or persecution arises because of the word, immediately he falls away.

Matthew 13:18-21 NASB

When Jesus taught this same parable in Mark chapter 4, He said that once the Word is sown in a man's heart, *Satan cometh immediately* to take away the Word which was sown (Mark 4:15). In both versions He says it is the evil one who comes and snatches away what has been sown.

AUTHORITY OF THE BELIEVER

As we have already determined, it is obvious why Satan must come and try to steal the Word: because the Word makes a person dangerous to him. The Word of God in your heart makes you dangerous to the adversary. Without it, you are no threat to him. But the moment you get the Word of God in your heart, you are bad news as far as Satan is concerned. You can stop his operations with it.

Many times people are afraid of the devil; but, in reality, he is afraid of us. We are the ones with the power. Jesus stripped Satan of his authority and his power in the bowels of this earth. The Bible says Jesus spoiled principalities and powers and made a show of them openly (Col. 2:15). He took from Satan the keys of death, hell, and the grave (Rev. 1:18). He stripped him of his armor, in which he trusted, and reduced him to zero.

Christ Jesus paralyzed Satan's death-dealing powers. When He was raised from the dead, He told His disciples: "All power is given unto me in heaven and in earth" (Matt. 28:18). Then He instructed them: "Go into all the world, and preach the Gospel to every creature. Cast out devils. Lay hands on the sick and they shall recover" (see Mark 16:15-18).

Who has authority in this earth? We do! We are the ones with the power. We are the ones the devil is afraid of. We shouldn't be afraid of him; he is afraid of us.

Don't misunderstand me, Satan is a worthy opponent. He's clever, but the main weapon he has is deception. The only way he can defeat you as a believer is to deceive you into putting down the Word. Satan's only hope of winning is to get you to quit operating in your authority, to quit using your power, to rob you of your joy. If he can deceive you, then he can defeat you.

DECEPTION IS SATAN'S MIGHTIEST WEAPON

Jesus said that once the Word is sown in a person's heart, the evil one comes to snatch it away. Now we know from the Scriptures that God's Word is the power of God. In Romans 1:16, the apostle Paul said, "For I am not ashamed of the gospel of Christ: for it is the power of God unto salvation."

It is amazing to me that a lot of Christians are still praying for power when it's right in front of them all the time. The Word of God is *the power of God unto salvation*.

I can assure you that as a book, the Bible is lifeless; but the moment you open that book, take the Word, and start injecting it into your spirit, then it becomes the Word of faith, the Word of power, the Word of health, the Word of life. It comes alive! It is impregnated with the power, life, and anointing of God. It makes you absolutely invincible. When you have this marvelous Word in your heart and are releasing it with your mouth, you become highly dangerous to the adversary. As far as Satan is concerned, *a Word-filled believer is his number-one enemy*.

You might ask, "Well, if I'm so powerful, how come the devil keeps beating me up?"

There is one reason: deception. He has deceived you. If Satan has been defeating you, it is because you have allowed it to happen. You are the one in authority in this earth, not Satan. You are the one with the power. You just haven't been exercising the authority that is yours as a child of God.

THAT YOUR JOY MIGHT BE FULL

*I am the true vine, and my Father is the husbandman.
Every branch in me that beareth not fruit he taketh
away: and every branch that beareth fruit, he purgeth
[prunes] it, that it may bring forth more fruit.*

*Now ye are clean through the word which I have spo-
ken unto you. Abide in me, and I in you. As the branch
cannot bear fruit of itself, except it abide in the vine; no
more can ye, except ye abide in me.*

*I am the vine, ye are the branches: He that abideth in
me, and I in him, the same bringeth forth much fruit: for
without me ye can do nothing.*

*If a man abide not in me, he is cast forth as a branch,
and is withered; and men gather them, and cast them into
the fire, and they are burned.*

*If ye abide in me, and my words abide in you, ye
shall ask what ye will, and it shall be done unto you.*

*Herein is my Father glorified, that ye bear much fruit;
so shall ye be my disciples.*

*As the Father hath loved me, so have I loved you:
continue ye in my love. If ye keep my commandments, ye*

shall abide in my love; even as I have kept my Father's commandments, and abide in his love.

These things have I spoken unto you, that my joy might remain in you, and that your joy might be full.

John 15:1-11

In verse 11, Jesus said, "These things have I spoken unto you, that my joy might remain in you, and that your joy might be full." What things did He speak unto us? He spoke revelations, the Word of God. Jesus said, "I don't do anything unless I see My Father do it; I don't say anything except what I hear My Father say." Evidently what Jesus is sharing with us is something God revealed to Him, something God inspired. In other words, what Jesus is sharing is the Word of God.

He says He is sharing these things with us so that His joy might be in us and that our joy might be *full*. The man who receives the Word of God will have joy—total joy, complete joy—because God's Word produces joy. It's the Gospel, the Good News.

Now it isn't good news to a poor man to be told that God loves poverty and wants him to remain poor. That's not the Gospel; that's a lie. God considers poverty a curse;

and according to Galatians 3:13, Christ has redeemed us from the curse.

Jesus spoke the Word of God to people to bring them good news, not bad news. He spoke the Word so that we might receive His joy and that our joy might be full. God's Word in your heart will produce joy in you, fullness of joy. Remember what Nehemiah said: "The joy of the Lord is your strength" (Neh. 8:10). God's Word produces joy, and joy produces strength.

Satan comes and tries to snatch the Word out of your heart. If he is successful, he gets your joy because joy is a product of something that was spoken by God. Because the joy of the Lord is your strength, when you lose your joy, you become weak. You become helpless, unable to overcome. You become an open target for Satan's attacks.

But remember what Jesus told us in John 16:22: "And ye now therefore have sorrow: but I will see you again, and your heart shall rejoice, and your joy no man taketh from you." We have seen that if no man can take your joy, neither can Satan. He does not have the legal right to do that, unless you give him that right.

Satan can't take your joy if you don't allow it. The only way he can take *anything* from you is by deceiving you into handing it over to him. For example, he will try to put symptoms of disease on your body and deceive you into believing that healing is not for you. If you fall for his deception, he'll not only get the Word out of your heart, he'll get the joy out of your heart, and you will lose your healing.

But he could not have made you sick if you hadn't let him do it. It took a conscious act of your will. You had to *will* to get deceived, *will* to get discouraged, *will* to let go of the Word. Satan can't take your joy if you're not willing to let him have it. If you will study your Bible very closely, you will find that God has provided every possible avenue for you to live victoriously. If you don't, it's your fault. You have nobody to blame but yourself.

THE GREAT PRETENDER

And there was war in heaven, Michael and his angels waging war with the dragon. The dragon and his angels waged war, and they were not strong enough, and there was no longer a place found for them in heaven. And the great dragon was thrown down, the serpent of old who is called the devil and Satan, who deceives the whole world; he was thrown down to the earth, and his angels were thrown down with him.

Revelation 12:7-9 NASB

The devil who is called Satan—that old serpent, the dragon—deceives the whole world. The only thing he has going for him is deception. Satan deceives. The devil is not a creator; he is a perverter. He has never created anything, and he never will. He can't create; all he can do is pervert something that God has already created. He perverted God's anointing upon him. He perverted it into iniquity.

You see, when he was Lucifer, the Bible tells us that God had created him perfect in all his ways, that he was full of wisdom and brightness and beauty, and that he was the anointed cherub. But then the Bible says iniquity was found in him (Ezek. 28:12-15).

Satan is a counterfeiter. For all that God has, the devil has a counterfeit.

The Word of God brings life; the word of Satan brings death.

The Word of God produces health; the word of Satan produces sickness and disease.

The Word of God begets prosperity; the word of Satan begets poverty.

God's Word sown in the heart of man brings forth life, joy, peace, abundance, and health; Satan's word sown in the heart of man brings forth death, misery, worry, lack, and disease.

It has taken Satan hundreds of years to get people to the place today that they will absolutely kill themselves in less than seventy years with the words of their mouths. Have you ever wondered why people in the Old Testament lived hundreds of years? They didn't know how to die. They hadn't been taught to die. Of course, God told Adam that if he disobeyed he would die. But Adam didn't even know what death was.

God created Adam to be an eternal being. God intended for Adam to live forever. He created him in His image, in His class, and never intended for him to die. But He warned him that if he partook of the fruit of the tree of knowledge of good and evil that he would surely die.

God was speaking, first of all, of a spiritual death. Adam was spiritually alive. After he committed high treason against God, he was "born again," but in a way opposite from the way you and I are born again. We are born into this life spiritually dead. When we make Jesus our Lord, we are born from death to life. Adam was already spiritually alive. When he committed high treason against God, he partook of another birth, and death was lodged in his heart. He became spiritually dead. Satan then became the illegitimate stepfather of all mankind. Adam died spiritually right then, and ultimately he died physically because the wages of sin is death. Sin will kill, because its wages are death (Rom. 6:23).

But Adam, being in God's class, didn't know how to die. It took over 900 years for the first man to die; and his descendants lived a long time, too. Why did they live so long? Because it took Satan years to come up with his own vocabulary—God's Word perverted. Satan was injecting death into his word while God was injecting life into His.

Through the centuries Satan has perfected this thing. He can kill a person now in a fraction of the time it took him to kill the first man.

ENSNARED BY OUR WORDS

The sad thing about all this is that half of the people in the Christian world have no idea that their own words are killing them. Listen to what we have come to accept as the "truth":

"I'm *taking* the flu." (You don't have to have it, but you're *taking* it.)

"I'm scared (starving, freezing, worried) *to death.*" (If you keep saying so, you certainly will be.)

"This inflation is *killing* me!" (You said it, brother!)

Satan has deceitfully, but cleverly, injected death into our vocabulary so that now we use it unconsciously as a manner of expression. Some folks get mad when you try to tell them that their words are ensnaring them, that they are taken captive by their own words. Solomon said, "Death and life are in the power of the tongue" (Prov. 18:21).

There are lots of people who still use the word *death* to express themselves: *I'm dying to go. That scared me to death. These kids are about to kill me.* Do you know what happens when you use words like that? Do you know what Satan does with that kind of testimony? He has a little imp assigned to you as a recorder or a secretary. This little imp follows you around recording everything you say. Every time you use words that are injected with death, fear, sickness, disease, poverty, lack, and want, they are recorded against you.

Jesus said that by your words you will be justified and by your words you will be condemned (Matt. 12:37). He said that you will give an account one day for every idle word that is spoken out of your mouth (Matt. 12:36). An idle word is a nonproductive word. Actually these negative words are counterproductive; they produce the opposite of what God wants for your life.

Every time you say, *That tickled me to death,* that little imp writes down: "tickled him/her to death." Then later you may say, *I'm just dying to go to that meeting.* The little imp records: "dying to go." A few days later you tell someone, *A car pulled right out in front of me today and scared me to death.* Down it goes in the imp's record book: "scared him/her to death." That little imp just keeps a list; and when the most opportune time comes (when you least expect it, so that you would never suspect that your words had anything to do with it), those words ensnare you.

The Bible says, "Put away from thee a froward mouth, and perverse lips put far from thee" (Prov. 4:24). Do you know what a "froward mouth" is? A froward mouth is a disobedient mouth. Many people think that "perverse lips" refers to cursing and obscenity. But do you know what perverse lips actually are? They are lips that speak anything contrary to "thus saith the Lord."

Satan is the perverter, and he has been trying to pervert the Word of God, which is the Word of life. It is Satan's plan and purpose to inject death into those words and to get us to use them all the time to express ourselves. If we continue to do so, we will eventually destroy our own lives with the very words of our mouths.

James said the tongue is evil, full of deadly poison, and "setteth on fire the course of nature" (James 3:6). In other words, James is telling us that the tongue is the source of many of our problems. He tells us in verse 2 that any man who can bridle his tongue can bridle his whole body. The problems we have with our bodies can be directly linked to what we're saying with our mouths.

Let me inject some good news here. Would you like to negate all the negative things you've been saying? Then make this commitment with me right now and erase those notes against you. Say this out loud:

Heavenly Father, forgive me for talking negatively, for speaking perverse things.

In the name of Jesus, I will not be ensnared by those things that have come from my mouth. I refuse to express myself with perverse things. In the name of Jesus, every negative thing, every perverse thing, every evil communication that has come out my mouth I negate with the Word of God.

Thank You, Father, for seeing to it that every negative thing I have spoken has been erased from this moment by the power of Your Word.

I no longer say I am scared to death because fear is of the enemy and I don't belong to him. I am a believer, full of faith and life. I'm not afraid because You are on my side. What can man do to me? If You are for me, who can be against me?

Satan, in the name of Jesus, you will not use anything I have said against me. My slate is clean.

Thank You, Lord, that it is done. Henceforth I will not speak Satan's lies, but I will speak forth Your truth—Your Word—and I will live the abundant, victorious life that You have provided for me through Jesus Christ, my Lord.

SPEAKING THE WORD

Satan is a perverter, a deceiver. He would love to deceive us and get the Word out of us, thus robbing us of our joy. If he can get our joy, then we don't have any foundation to stand on. It's hard to enter into warfare with the enemy when you're discouraged, when you've lost your joy.

But when you stand with your feet firmly planted, with your body covered by the whole armor of God, with the sword of the Spirit—the Word of the Living God—coming out of your mouth, then you will be victorious over *every* circumstance of life.

Though it may look as if everything around you is falling apart and all hell is breaking loose, the battle isn't over as long as you have the joy of the Lord. You have an opportunity to win as long as you still have that joy and are still speaking that Word.

Anybody who has ever made an attempt to live by God's Word has had an opportunity to fail. You will, too! You will have opportunity to compromise, to fold up and quit. There will be times when it feels as though all the world and half the Christians are against you. There will be moments when it seems that you have stood as long as you possibly can and can't stand any longer.

The apostle Paul said the shield of faith is used to quench *every* fiery dart of the evil one (Eph. 6:16). There have been times when I have felt as though my shield was so full of darts that I couldn't hold it up anymore. (That old shield gets heavy when it's full of darts!)

Sometimes the pressure would be so strong, it felt like my helmet was about to fall off, that the rivets had popped out of my breastplate, that the soles of my Gospel shoes were slick. It seemed that I couldn't keep my belt of truth up any longer. My sword seemed so dull it wouldn't cut hot butter. Maybe you've been in that situation, too.

When you first start out, you strap on that armor and sword, then you stand bold as the Lion of the tribe of Judah—the Word coming out your mouth with sharpness: "In the name of Jesus, I am healed by His stripes!" But after you've stood on the Word for about a week, the shield begins to get heavy and your sword gets dull. Your testimony tends to change from "I'm healed!" to "Oh, I hope I'm healed."

You stand and resist Satan's darts until you think, *Dear God, if he throws one more dart, I don't think I can stand it.*

Then suddenly you can hear it coming through the breeze, sounding like a missile. He has kept the best weapon he's got in reserve, and that thing has been launched directly at you at your weakest moment. You start thinking, *Oh, Lord, it's not only going to get my shield, it's going to come through my breastplate and knock me over! I've had it!*

You hear it coming closer and closer. Then when you think all is lost, the Holy Ghost begins to say to you, "Rejoice! You have the devil right where you want him!"

"I do?"

"Lift up your head and rejoice. The devil is running scared."

"He is?"

"Straighten yourself up; you've won!"

"I have?"

"That's right. You have!"

The Lord told me a secret about the devil, and I'm going to pass it on to you. (Satan doesn't like for me to tell this, but here goes anyway.) I was in that kind of situation one time and I thought, *If one more dart lands, I think I'm going to fall.* Then I heard it coming toward me. I could see the circumstances out there lining up for this dart, and it was going to be a monster. I thought for sure I was gone.

But then the Lord said to me, "Son, lift up your hands and begin to rejoice because you have the devil right where you want him. This is what you've been waiting for. You have the devil running scared. You're a winner now; the manifestation is right around the corner. Don't give up now. Son, don't you realize that when you're under the most severe pressure for standing on My Word, that is a good indication that the devil has just fired his best shot? If that one doesn't get you, he's through!"

When I heard that bit of information, I said, "Devil, I've got you right where I want you!"

You need to realize that the only way Satan can defeat you is by deceiving you into letting go of the Word. If you will stand firm and speak forth that Word with faith, and power, and strength, Satan has no chance; you have won the victory against him. Speak the Word.

BINDING THE DECEIVER

Then I saw an angel coming down from heaven, holding the key of the abyss and a great chain in his hand. And he laid hold of the dragon, the serpent of old, who is the devil and Satan, and bound him for a thousand

*years; and he threw him into the abyss, and shut it and
sealed it over him, so that he would not deceive the
nations any longer.*

Revelation 20:1-3 NASB

I want you to notice that as long as Satan was bound,
he could not deceive. He is a deceiver by nature. That's
his mightiest weapon—deception. But as long as he was
bound, he could not deceive anyone.

Notice verses 7 and 8 (NASB): "And when the thousand years are completed, Satan will be released from his
prison, and will come out to deceive."

When Satan is bound, he can't deceive. But when he
is loosed and running free, he can. It's automatic.

Well, I have some good news for you! *You don't have
to wait until the thousand-year reign to bind the devil. You can
do it right now!* Jesus said whatever you bind on earth will
be bound in heaven and whatever you loose on earth will
be loosed in heaven (Matt. 16:19). If you will bind Satan,
he can't deceive.

Now let me show you something about deception.
There are people who have yielded their money or
other valuables to someone who came up behind them

and stuck a finger in their back. Those poor folks were deceived. They assumed that what they felt was a gun. I read an article about a bank that yielded $50,000 to a guy with a "gun" in his coat pocket. They later found out that the only thing he had in his pocket was his hand.

Do you see how helpless people become when they are deceived? That's exactly what the devil does—he deceives. Satan is nothing but a coward.

You may say, "But, Brother, the Bible says he is a roaring lion seeking whom he may devour." It doesn't say he *is* a lion. It says, "Your adversary the devil, *as a roaring lion,* walketh about, seeking whom he may devour" (1 Pet. 5:8). Satan is not a lion; he just tries to act like one! If you will look at him closely, you will see that he is a lion with no teeth. Jesus pulled his teeth in the bowels of the earth! All he can do now is prowl around and roar. If you fall for that roar, he's got you. Have you ever been hurt by a dog with no teeth?

I like what Charles Capps says: "The devil doesn't even need teeth where some Christians are concerned. They are so pliable and spineless that he can just gum them to death!"

The devil isn't a lion; all he can do is roar like one and try to frighten you into surrendering to him. The Bible says, "The righteous are bold as a lion" (Prov. 28:1). When Satan starts to roar at you, turn around and roar back at him. He will run off like a whipped kitten because *you* are the one with the authority. You are a joint-heir with the Lion of the tribe of Judah. Satan is not the lion—*you* are!

THREE TYPES OF DECEPTION

Now let me show you something about deception. Deception comes in three basic forms: *statement, influence,* and *appearance.*

Deception by Statement

One way Satan attempts to deceive people is through statement. By this I mean simply the mingling together of God's Word with a false idea. You can easily be deceived by this if you are not careful.

Did you know that all false teaching is based on the Scriptures? Let me make this a little clearer. Every false teaching is based on some Scripture that has been distorted. The Body of Christ is not going to fall for anything that doesn't have a verse of Scripture connected to it.

For example, if someone told you that suicide is of God, you wouldn't believe it. But some people would fall for it if that person had a Scripture verse to support it. You can take Scriptures out of context, come up with any kind of doctrine, and some poor soul will believe it. It is entirely possible for someone to stand up and preach, "'Suicide is of God.' The Bible says so. Matthew 27:5 says, 'Judas went and hanged himself,' and in Luke 10:37, Jesus says, 'Go, and do thou likewise.'"

So here you have it: the suicide doctrine! That is *deception by statement*. There are always people who will fall for that sort of thing because they are not established in the Word.

This is how Satan managed to deceive Eve in the Garden. When Eve was tempted by the serpent, she said, "But God said that if we eat of the fruit of this tree, we will surely die" (see Gen. 3:3). What did Satan say to her? "Hath God said?" (Gen. 3:1). He added to God's Word, deceiving her into committing sin.

You know, this is one of the dirtiest tricks the devil pulls on believers. His vilest trick of deception is to take some Scripture, change its meaning, and get a believer to go for it. The only way he can deceive a believer is to distort the Scriptures.

He tried to do this with Jesus. After Jesus had been on the mount fasting for forty days and nights, Satan came to tempt Him. He said, "If thou be the Son of God, command that these stones be made bread" (Matt. 4:3). Notice what Jesus did. His life was based on the Word. He said, "It is written, Man shall not live by bread alone, but by every word that proceedeth out of the mouth of God" (Matt. 4:4).

That answer showed the devil right away, "Oh, we've got one of those Word people here, one of those faith guys. We're not going to be able to fool Him by suggestion; we're going to have to deceive Him by statement. We'll distort the Scriptures."

So Satan took Jesus up to the pinnacle of the temple and said to Him, "If thou be the Son of God, cast thyself down: for it is written…" (Matt. 4:6). He took a verse of Scripture and quoted it, trying to get Jesus to believe that as long as He was standing on a Scripture, He could cast Himself down from the temple and God would protect Him.

Do you know what the devil was trying to do? He was trying to get Jesus to commit suicide by standing on the Scriptures. But his trick didn't work. Jesus saw through that right away. He answered Satan, "Thou shalt not tempt the Lord thy God" (Matt. 4:7).

So Satan attempts to deceive believers by statement, by distorting the Scriptures. This wouldn't work with Jesus because He not only knew the Word, He also had the spiritual perception and wisdom to rightly divide the word of truth (2 Tim. 2:15). And so must we if we are to avoid being deceived in this way.

Deception by Influence

Another form of deception used by Satan is *deception by influence.* By this I simply mean past experience. The devil loves to deceive people by reminding them, "Remember the last time you tried to act on that Scripture? What happened? You really blew it!" He drags up past failures to influence people not to act on faith in the Word.

Or he may use the negative reaction of others to influence you to doubt and lose faith. Let me give you an example. Suppose you are making your stand on the Word for finances, saying, "In the name of Jesus Christ, my God supplies all my need according to His riches in glory by Christ Jesus." About that time some lovely, sincere (but sincerely wrong) Christian crosses your path and asks, "How are you doing, Brother? How are your finances?"

"Thank God, in the name of Jesus, I believe my needs are met."

"Oh, really? You know, Sister Doodad confessed that for seven weeks, and they repossessed everything she had. She lost her home and everything. She's living down there with Sister So-and-So now."

That's what the devil delights in doing. He just loves to drag up past experiences—either yours or someone else's—and deceive you into believing that it isn't going to work for you. He is trying to steal the Word from your heart.

Have you ever noticed how an evil report can get your joy—if you allow it to? You can be on top of the world with a dance in your step. Then somebody crosses your path with a bad story. If you don't watch, it will get your joy. You'll come down off that cloud like a lead balloon. Satan will use that negative influence to rob you of your joy. He will deceive you, and he will continue to do so if you let him.

Deception by Appearance

Perhaps Satan's most effective means of deceiving people is through appearance. Things appear to be something they are not. Many people fall for these appearances: "Well, it looked like I was going to lose." As Christians we should know that things are not always the way they appear.

One time when Jesus had ministered to a multitude of people, He told His disciples to get into their boat and go to the other side of the lake. Jesus dismissed the crowd then went up into a mountain to pray. In a little while there was a storm on the lake, and Jesus came down from the mountain. When He realized that His disciples were about to drown, He went to them, walking on the water.

Now these men were already filled with fear. If you'll notice, the Bible never says, "And they cried out in faith!"

No, it's always fear that moved them to that extreme. They were afraid. The storm was raging. The waves were beating against the ship. They were about to drown.

When they saw Jesus walking on the water, they were more frightened than ever because they thought it was a ghost. They cried out for fear. But Jesus said to them, "Be of good cheer; it is I; be not afraid" (Matt. 14:27). Peter walked to the edge of the ship and said, "Lord, if it be thou, bid me come unto thee on the water" (Matt. 14:28). "And he said, Come" (Matt. 14:29).

So Peter stepped out of the boat and walked on the water. Many people read this account and think that the moment Peter stepped out of the boat, he began to sink. He did not. The Bible says he stepped out of the boat and walked on the water toward Jesus (Matt. 14:29). The man was doing it! He was a success. But I want you to know that Peter had to see himself doing that before he would ever get out of the boat.

Peter was operating in faith. He stepped out of the boat while the storm was still raging. The boat was still pitching back and forth, but Peter stepped out on the storm-tossed water and started walking to Jesus. He was a success—for a while.

But then notice what the Bible says: "When he saw the wind boisterous, he was afraid; and beginning to sink, he cried, saying, Lord, save me" (Matt. 14:30). Satan deceived Peter through appearances. He deceived Peter into thinking, *You can't walk on water when it's windy!* What else could he have been thinking? The wind never crossed his mind until he looked. Then he thought, *This is ridiculous! You can't do this when there's wind!*

You see, it *appeared* to Peter that he shouldn't be able to do what he was doing. Do you see how Satan *caused deception through appearance?* It *appeared* that Peter couldn't do this thing. When he got his eyes off the Word and onto the problem, what happened? He began to cry out for fear again. The Word had been stolen out of his heart. His joy was gone. He was deprived of confidence. He began to doubt. He began to look at the wind, to look at the problem. He accepted defeat and began to sink.

It is a beautiful story how Jesus reached down, grabbed Peter before he sank, pulled him back up, put His arms around him, walked him back to the ship, rebuked the wind, and then said, "Peter, why did you doubt?" (see Matt. 14:31). It is beautiful how the Lord will save you right at the last minute. I've heard some beautiful sermons about how the Lord will deliver you just in the nick of time, right from the jaws of hell. That's great, but it wasn't God's best. Who wants to always be delivered at the last minute? Why don't we win some? Why don't we win in style a few times?

I am convinced that Jesus wanted Peter to walk out there on the water, keeping his eyes on Jesus, and not let circumstances deceive him into believing that he couldn't do it. Jesus wanted Peter to keep walking to Him, then they would walk back to the ship together. When Peter was back in the ship, he could have said to the others, "Hey, you can do it, too!" And they could have, had they believed and acted on that faith.

But they were all deceived. They took things at face value, at the way they appeared. That was Peter's mistake—looking at things as they seemed to be instead of standing on God's Word. He was deceived.

BE NOT DECEIVED

You will do some stupid things sometimes when you allow yourself to be deceived. You forget everything you know about the Word. You become irrational. When you are afraid, everything you know about the Word suddenly flies out the window and you do foolish things.

That's exactly what Satan wants you to do. He wants your joy, and he wants it badly. As long as you have joy in your heart, you're a threat to him. God's Word and the joy that is produced by the Word had been lodged in your heart. The only way Satan can successfully get it out is through deception. He has to deceive you in some way.

If he can't deceive you, he can't get the Word.

If he can't get the Word, he can't get your joy.

If he can't get your joy, he can't get your strength.

If he can't get your strength, then you are a winner in everything you set your hand to.

The apostle Paul tells us in Galatians 6:7, "Be not deceived." If Satan cannot deceive you, he cannot stop you from living a life of abundance, peace, and victory.

If Satan can't steal your joy,

…he can't keep your goods.

…he can't defeat you.

…he can't deceive you.

PRAYER OF SALVATION

God loves you—no matter who you are, no matter what your past. God loves you so much that He gave His one and only begotten Son for you. The Bible tells us that "whoever believes in him shall not perish but have eternal life" (John 3:16 NIV). Jesus laid down His life and rose again so that we could spend eternity with Him in heaven and experience His absolute best on earth. If you would like to receive Jesus into your life, say the following prayer out loud and mean it from your heart.

Heavenly Father, I come to You admitting that I am a sinner. Right now, I choose to turn away from sin, and I ask You to cleanse me of all unrighteousness. I believe that Your Son, Jesus, died on the cross to take away my sins. I also believe that He rose again from the dead so that I might be forgiven of my sins and made righteous through faith in Him. I call upon the name of Jesus Christ to be the Savior and Lord of my life. Jesus, I choose to follow You and ask that You fill me with the power of the Holy Spirit. I declare that right now I am a child of God. I am free from sin and full of the righteousness of God. I am saved in Jesus' name. Amen.

HERE'S A SNEAK PEEK FROM *IF SATAN CAN'T STEAL YOUR DREAMS...*

1

SATAN TARGETS YOUR DREAMS

It would be wonderful if God just laid out the whole picture of your life and said, "Now, here's where you're going; here's everything that's going to happen before you get there; here's each day of your life for the next fifteen years; and here's how it's going to turn out." However, if He did that, our lives wouldn't require faith.

God is not going to lay everything out for you. He'll give you one piece of the puzzle at a time. Each piece connected to the other piece will create a perfect picture of God's plan for your life. But those pieces must be connected together by faith in His Word. Every step you take must be a step of faith.

Psalm 37:23 says, "The steps of a good man are ordered by the Lord." In this journey of faith, you're going to have to be very sensitive to God. Like Abraham, you must take the steps God ordains and directs so you'll end up at the destination to which He has called you.

> *By faith he* [Abraham] *sojourned in the land of promise, as in a strange country, dwelling in tabernacles with Isaac and Jacob, the heirs with him of the same promise: for he looked for a city which hath foundations, whose builder and maker is God.*

> Hebrews 11:9-10

As you will see later in this book, Abraham didn't know where he was going, but he was always looking. Are you looking today? Are you looking for the manifestations of what God has promised? Are you anticipating the fulfillment? Are you laying aside all doubts and expecting God's every promise to happen? Right now, God is building something in your life. It is your job to look for what is built and made by God. In order to do this, you have to create a proper atmosphere and refuse to fear anything that would stand in your way—even failure.

CREATING AN ATMOSPHERE FOR YOUR DREAMS

There are things you can do to create a proper atmosphere for your dream, and there are also things that will create an improper atmosphere. What kind of atmosphere do you live in? Is there an atmosphere of faith? Is there an atmosphere of trust and belief? If so, then you will attract miracles, because faith moves God. While fear activates the adversary, faith activates God.

The Bible says that without faith it is impossible to please God (Heb. 11:6). Therefore, a faith atmosphere causes our God-given dreams to come to pass. A fear atmosphere only hinders them. Our dreams are fulfilled by faith.

Usually, however, the thing many people fear in life the most is failure. They fear that if they step out in their dreams, everything will fall apart.

Even if it looks as if your manifestation will never come to pass, you must allow faith and confidence to rise up within you. You must have a resolve to depend on and have faith in God alone—even if there is opposition.

Micah faced such opposition, but take a look at his declaration when he faced it:

Therefore I will look unto the Lord; I will wait for the God of my salvation: my God will hear me. Rejoice not against me, O mine enemy: when I fall, I shall arise; when I sit in darkness, the Lord shall be a light unto me.

Micah 7:7-8

"I will look unto the Lord. I will wait for the God of my salvation. My God will hear me." That's how God wants His children to speak. God always rejoices with you when you show the confidence to overcome adversity.

Satan is the one who rejoices *against* you, especially when you make mistakes. However, when he tries to get you to wallow in self-doubt, remember this: No one is without mistake. We've all stumbled. We've all fallen at some time or another. In fact, you probably will make a few more mistakes along the way. You have to remember it's not failure to fall. It's only failure to stay down.

Micah said, "when I fall, I shall arise." There will come a place and a time in your life when you finally have to decide once and for all that if you fall, you will arise again no matter how far you have fallen.

Look at what the Bible says in Psalm 37:23-24.

The steps of a good man are ordered by the Lord: and he delighteth in his way. Though he fall, he shall not be utterly cast down: for the Lord upholdeth him with his hand.

The devil expects you to quit. He wants you to say, "Where is God?" He wants you to get discouraged and fearful of stepping out into the biggest dreams and desires of your life. He wants you to be afraid of failure.

However, God wants you to get it into your spirit that if you fall, it is not over. He wants you to determine that no matter how many times you fall, with the support of His hand, you shall arise.

All of us have dreams and desires that we would like to see happen in our lives. Yet it seems as if all of the things we desire from God are beyond our natural ability to accomplish.

You are about to learn some life-changing principles that will help to propel you into all that you are to be. I want to help you to recapture the dream that the thief may have stolen from you. The Scripture tells us:

> *The thief cometh not, but for to steal, and to kill, and to destroy: I am come that they might have life, and that they might have it more abundantly.*

> John 10:10

God wants us all to live the abundant life, to walk in prosperity and live in His absolute best at all times. Why, then, does it seem that some believers walk in abundance while others never seem to?

There is a God (the one true God) who promises to bring us abundance, but there is also a thief who wants to steal, kill, and destroy everything that God has promised us. Satan's goal is to steal our dreams because he knows that if he can do that, he can destroy our future. We have to remember that if Satan can't steal our dreams, he can't take our future! It's up to us to stop him from stealing our dreams.

Did you know that Satan wants to steal your dreams? It's true. You are a threat to him as long as you continue to pursue all that God has for you. If you choose to walk in the abundance that God has promised you, the devil will always try to come and steal away everything you have—including your dreams.

However, you don't need to worry. Although the devil is a thief, you are a partaker of abundant life. Because Jesus is with you, in you, and able to deliver you, there is nothing for you to be concerned about when the oppressor comes.

When we read the book of Acts, we learn that "God anointed Jesus of Nazareth with the Holy Ghost and with power: who went about doing good, and healing all that were oppressed of the devil; for God was with him" (Acts 10:38). Jesus healed all who were oppressed of the devil—*all!* That includes you.

If Satan is challenging and oppressing you, it doesn't mean defeat. It could be a clear sign that you are doing something that is making him afraid. Notice I said that Satan is afraid, not you. The devil wants to stop you because he is afraid if you win, then the more you will talk about his defeat.

One of the methods the devil uses to steal the dreams of the believer is to lie. The Bible tells us that Satan abides "not in the truth, because there is no truth in him. When he speaketh a lie, he speaketh of his own: for he is a liar, and the father of it" (John 8:44).

Satan is the father of lies. That means everything he says to you is a lie. When he tells you that you will never see a financial breakthrough in your life, it is a lie. When he tells you that you cannot be healed, it is a lie. When he tells you that you will never fulfill your dreams, it is a lie. In fact, John 8:44 is *proof* that these are lies.

Furthermore, the same Bible that tells you that Satan is the father of lies also tells you that God *cannot* lie! Paul spoke of this in Titus:

Paul, a servant of God, and an apostle of Jesus Christ, according to the faith of God's elect, and the acknowledging of the truth which is after godliness; in hope of eternal life, which God, that cannot lie, promised before the world began.

Titus 1:1-2

Let's look at the entire truth of this matter. The Bible says that Satan is the father of lies. The Bible also says that God *cannot* lie. This means that while everything that Satan says about you is a lie, everything that God says about you is true. If God says that you are healed, then you are healed (Isa. 53:5). If He says that you are to live an abundant life, then it is so. If He has told you that He is able to do exceedingly, abundantly above all that you can ever ask or think, then He is (Eph. 3:20).

Many believers easily acknowledge that the devil is a liar but forget that everything God says is true. Perhaps you've heard the saying, "God said it; I believe it; that settles it." I have to slightly disagree with that statement. This is the way I see it: God said it, and that settles it! It is settled whether we believe it or not. Our believing it will only be to our advantage.

FEAR—SATAN'S COUNTERFEIT TO FAITH

The advantage of believing is the confidence that is produced when you believe. When you believe what God says, there is no need to be afraid of what the devil says. Fear is not a product of anything God says; the product of God's Word is faith, as Romans 10:17 tells us: "So then faith cometh by hearing, and hearing by the word of God."

When we consistently listen to the Word of God, faith is produced. On the other hand, when we listen to the voice of the devil, fear is produced. The reason is that fear opposes faith. It is the spiritual force that causes Satan to produce the greatest possible damage.

Three words should never come out of the mouth of the believer. Those three words are: "I am afraid." These words immediately put to action the works of the adversary.

That's what the devil wants you to say when you're under pressure and it looks as if everything you're going through is impossible to overcome. The first thing the devil wants you to do is to question God's faithfulness. The devil loves it when Christians start to question God, and the strongest way you can question God's integrity is to say that you are afraid.

The devil loves to hear words of fear come out of the mouths of believers because it means he has successfully gotten them to oppose their own nature. A believer naturally believes; it is unnatural for a believer to walk in unbelief. The most natural thing for the children of God to do is to trust their Father.

Anybody who does not trust one's father either has a father who cannot be depended upon or has believed lies about him. Perhaps you grew up with a father who couldn't be trusted. If that is the case, it would be understandable why you have no confidence in that father. However, your heavenly Father cannot lie. He can be trusted. The Bible tells us:

God is not a man, that he should lie; neither the son of man, that he should repent: hath he said, and shall he not do it? or hath he spoken, and shall he not make it good?

Numbers 23:19

It is impossible for God to lie. He can be trusted.

If you're having a problem trusting the Father God, perhaps you need to get to know Him better. Whatever He says will be done. He will make good on all of the promises He has spoken out of His mouth and written in His Word.

Contrarily, the devil will take every measure to lie to you about God. Here is a simple rule of thumb for living by faith: Whenever the devil tells you something, believe the opposite. Everything the devil says is a lie. When he starts saying there is no way out of your current situation, it's a lie. When he tells you God is not hearing your prayer, it's a lie.

It is impossible for Satan to tell the truth. The next time he tells you something, don't cry. Just laugh! He cannot help himself. Everything he says is a lie.

The devil may try to tell you that your children will never get saved. He may say that he is going to destroy your marriage. Those things are lies designed to bring fear into your life to oppose the faith that is in your heart.

According to Hebrews 11:1, "faith is the substance of things hoped for." Yet fear is the substance of things dreaded. It is important to remember that when God speaks, faith comes. On the other hand, when Satan speaks, fear comes—if you believe what he says.

THE THING I HAVE GREATLY "FAITHED"

Just as you must mix faith with what God says in order to give His Word substance, you must mix fear with what the devil says in order to give his words substance. This is exactly what happened with Job.

> *For the thing which I greatly feared is come upon me,*
> *and that which I was afraid of is come unto me.*
>
> Job 3:25

The very thing Job feared came upon him. In fact, the Scripture tells us that Job "greatly" feared. His fear activated the will of the devil. As a result, Job lost everything he had. The same thing can happen to anyone who listens to and believes what the devil says.

If something you greatly fear can come upon you, then it stands to reason that something you greatly "faith" can come upon you. The next time someone asks you why you are living in so much victory, you can tell them, "That which I greatly *faithed* came upon me."

The devil will always tell you things that are in direct opposition to the promises of God. If God says in His Word that you are prosperous, the devil will tell you that you are broke. If God says that you are healed, the devil will say that you are sick (3 John 1:2). If God tells you that great peace shall be upon your household, you can always count on the devil to try to bring worry (Isa. 32:18). He tells you lies to try to cause you to respond in fear rather than faith. Although the things he says are lies, he wants you to believe them and respond in fear so that substance can be added to those lies.

If you want all that God has for you, fear cannot be a part of your life. With faith in God, there is nothing to be afraid of.

CONQUER FEAR BY CONFRONTING IT

No one of us is born with a spirit of fear. Nor is it something given to us from God. The Bible says, "For God hath not given us the spirit of fear; but of power, and of love, and of a sound mind" (2 Tim. 1:7). If you're not born with fear and God did not give you fear, then someone had to teach you to fear.

I have a sister who is about four years younger than I am. When I was a young boy, I used to notice my little sister crawling into dark rooms around the house. I would tell her, "Don't ever let me catch you crawling in those dark rooms again. It's terrible in there. It's scary!" After a while, she wouldn't crawl into dark rooms—only because I'd taught her to be afraid.

Fear comes by hearing. Some people are afraid of flying in airplanes because they've heard about crashes. Yet cars also crash. Will you stop driving? In fact, people get hurt all the time simply by walking down the street. Will you stop walking? Will you just stay in bed all day? But some people die in bed.

If you keep listening, the devil will back you into a corner until you are absolutely tormented by fear. He'll begin with something that is not even reasonable; then as you start believing his lies, fear will increase.

If you can develop faith, then you can also develop fear. Just as you develop faith by hearing, you can develop fear by hearing. Remember, Romans 10:17 says, "So then faith cometh by hearing, and hearing by the word of God."

Too many people lean on what the devil says and end up being controlled by fear. If we lean on what God says, it brings faith, and faith gives us the ability to conquer everything that comes our way.

I encourage you today to consume your life with the Word of God. Listen to faith-building tapes every day. Read your Bible—not as a religious duty, but as a faith-developing tool to help you achieve your dreams. Spend time in the presence of God. Fear will leave and faith will come.

Right now, you may feel as if you're at the bottom of the barrel. You may feel as if everything you've done has amounted to nothing. You may have been told that you have fallen too far down to get back up. Now is the time to look to the Word and declare, "When I fall, I shall arise!" I don't care how far down you are, you can arise. Get back up and allow God to help you recapture your dream.

2

IT'S TIME TO RECAPTURE YOUR DREAMS

Many people have dreams for their lives, but few ever see them come to pass. Will your dreams be fulfilled, or will they be lost forever? The answer will be determined by your attitude. Fulfillment is the result of an aggressive, positive attitude; failure is the result of a passive, negative attitude.

There are three types of people in this world:

1. Aggressive—people who make things happen;
2. Passive—people who hope things might happen;
3. Wonderers—people who wonder, "What happened?"

Determine that you will be the one who makes things happen!

Since you've become a believer, I am sure that God has given you some dreams. You have probably followed through with some dreams and let go of others. I challenge you to give some thought to the dreams that God has given you. Write them down, aggressively pursue their fulfillment, and check them off as they come to pass. Don't just settle for a life with no purpose. Even though it may appear that your dream may never come to pass, don't sit by and allow the devil to steal it from you.

POSSESSING YOUR VISION

When you know that you've heard from God and have received direction from Him, zeal rises up on the inside of you. There's just something about hearing from God: Once you receive it, you can never again be passive about what He has told you to do.

Once you realize that you have authority in the name of Jesus, you will become bold in your stand of faith. Once you find out that by His stripes you were healed, you can no longer remain passive about sickness. Revelation knowledge concerning your right to live in health demands that you attack that sickness with the authority that He has given you through His Word.

We have a covenant with God, which promises that He will take care of us, so we cannot be passive about what is rightfully ours. Likewise, once you find out that God has a purpose for your life, you must go after it! You have to fulfill what God has called you to do. You must pursue His dream for your life.

Acts 3:19-21 says:

Repent ye therefore, and be converted, that your sins may be blotted out, when the times of refreshing shall come from the presence of the Lord. And he shall send Jesus Christ, which before was preached unto you: whom the heaven must receive until the times of restitution of all things, which God hath spoken by the mouth of all his holy prophets since the world began.

God is ready to restore some things in your life today. He wants to restore everything that Satan has stolen from you, including your dreams.

If you're not winning yet, don't give up! God is not through with you. If you've made mistakes and had setbacks, then just remember that God is the God of restoration.

It's time to recapture our divine destiny. We need to recapture our sense of purpose. If we are not careful, we can lose our confidence that we've heard from God.

It is time to take back what the devil has tried to take away from you. The devil thinks that he can take away what God has promised you, but he does not have the authority to do so. God has given you the authority to possess what is yours. So, don't give up!

PAINTING AN IMAGE

Every dream that God drops in your heart begins with a picture of that dream before it becomes a reality. In other words, you have to see it on the inside. When you study the Bible and you discover a promise from God, that promise is designed by the Holy Spirit to be painted on the inside of you.

Words create images. The Word of God says in 3 John 1:2, "I wish above all things that thou mayest prosper and be in health." The Holy Spirit will take that Scripture, those God-inspired words, and create an image on the inside of you of prosperity and health coming into your life.

You will begin to see yourself with health and prosperity. Your image will become perfected through constant fellowship and communion with the Holy Spirit. It will become more real to you than what is happening on the outside.

The Bible says, "As he [a man] thinketh in his heart, so is he" (Prov. 23:7). God's Word is designed to paint images. I like to say it this way: Your heart is the canvas, the Holy Spirit is the Artist, and the Word of God is the oil. As you fellowship with God, the Holy Spirit will paint an image on the canvas of your heart of how God sees you—not as the world sees you.

Revelation knowledge of God's Word paints images in your heart of who you are, what you are, and what you are entitled to as a child of God. That's why God gave us His Word. The Word of God will paint an image on the inside of your heart concerning your purpose.

In Acts chapter 26, the apostle Paul boldly and authoritatively declared his purpose to King Agrippa.

He was able to do that because God's Word had been revealed to him.

And when we were all fallen to the earth, I heard a voice speaking unto me, and saying in the Hebrew tongue, Saul, Saul, why persecutest thou me? it is hard for thee to kick against the pricks.

And I said, Who art thou, Lord? And he said, I am Jesus whom thou persecutest. But rise, and stand upon thy feet: for I have appeared unto thee for this purpose.

Acts 26:14-16

Jesus told Paul that He had appeared to him for a particular purpose. Jesus has a special purpose for your life as well. Jesus talks to you through the Word, by His Spirit. He speaks to you in order to give you purpose.

This is why it is important to spend time with Jesus. He has a purpose for each one of us, but the only way to know that purpose is to spend time with Him. As you fellowship with Him, you will begin to have clear understanding of what He wants you to do with your life.

KEEPING THE RIGHT COMPANY

Have you ever seen people who seem to have no goals, no dreams, no vision, and no purpose? These are not the kind of people you want to keep company with. If you're not watchful, they will pull you away from your dream. They will hinder you from fulfilling your purpose.

To create the proper atmosphere for your dreams to become a reality, you must associate with the right people. Don't share your dreams with nondreamers. Don't share "impossible things" with people who do not believe that all things are possible to those who believe. As Proverbs 13:20 says, you need to walk with the right people: "He that walketh with wise men shall be wise: but a companion of fools shall be destroyed."

Associating with the right kind of people creates the right atmosphere for success. Some people in your life might feel called to convince you that you didn't hear from God or that what you heard will never come to pass. Even some family members may try to talk you out of everything God has told you.

I remember one time when our ministry was involved in a building project and the devil fought us over it day and night. He kept saying that we would never be able to finish the project. I had been invited to preach in a meeting in Tulsa, Oklahoma, so instead of staying where I normally stayed, I decided to get a hotel room directly across from the campus of Oral Roberts University, and I requested a room with a view.

I checked into my hotel room, opened the drapes, pulled my chair right up in front of the window, and sat for hours looking out at that campus. I told the devil, "Just as faith built this campus, faith will build what God wants me to build."

Now notice that I didn't go look for people who would agree with the devil and tell me that it was impossible. If I had done that, it's highly probable that they would have tried to rob me of my dream and pull me down to their level. I didn't need that. I was building something that was impossible. I needed to be stirred up and encouraged. I needed an atmosphere of faith, not of doubt.

Have you ever noticed that the non-dreamers usually outnumber the dreamers? That means you're going to have to be very selective about your companionships. Your determination to keep the right company may cost you some so-called friends. Remember, though, that the companion of fools will be destroyed. If you walk around with foolish people and non-dreamers, you're going to get hurt. They will steal your dream right out of your heart.

Determine that you're going to associate with the right kind of people who will help create a proper atmosphere for your dreams to come true. Don't run around with faithless people. Don't expose your dreams to people who never dream. Fellowship with those who believe and practice in their own lives the reality that all things are possible to those who believe!

LETTING GO OF THE DREAM

People let go of their dreams for many reasons. Many times, adversity and the opinions of others can cause people to lose sight of what God has called them to do. This is why it is so important to possess a spirit of faith.

Paul captured his divine purpose in his encounter with Jesus, who plainly told him:

Stand upon thy feet: for I have appeared unto thee for this purpose, to make thee a minister and a witness both of these things which thou hast seen, and of those things in the which I will appear unto thee.

Acts 26:16

Jesus told Paul that He appeared to him "for this purpose"—to make Paul a minister. Just as in Paul's case,
when God gives you a purpose, He is also the One who
will cause it to come to pass. Your responsibility is to hold
on to it no matter how impossible it may appear to be.

Every Christian, whether in the ministry or not, has
a purpose and a dream. We all have a God-given destiny.
The spirit of faith will help us reach that destiny.

I want to challenge you once again to give some
thought to the dreams that God has given you. Write
them down. Remember to also write down the dreams
that you may have let go of. Recapture them so that God
can bring them to pass. Determine that you will never let
go of what God has spoken to you.

DON'T LET GO OF THE SEEDS YOU HAVE SOWN

The Lord dealt with me about a few things at a time
when I had almost lost my motivation to fulfill one of my
dreams. I was trying to recover from a number of setbacks
at the time.

I was in a meeting one night and the Spirit of God placed it in my heart to give my airplane to another minister. I obeyed Him and did what He had told me to do. At that time, God had promised me a bigger, better, and faster airplane. However, I had let go of that dream when some things happened that resulted in a lot of financial pressure. When you're barely making ends meet, the last thing you want to think about is a bigger airplane. You simply don't need a bigger airplane when you're trying to stay afloat. Buying and owning it is not all the expense; it costs a lot of money to maintain it. This is why I had let go of my dream. In times like those, you don't want God to talk about expanding. What you want is for somebody to bring you some relief.

During this time, my wife and I wouldn't even discuss a new airplane, or anything else that would demand more money. Yet we knew that God wanted us to grow.

It wasn't long before the Holy Spirit began to remind us of what had been promised to us, so we slowly began to talk about it again. We began to speak about our dream in relation to the seeds that we had already sown. We decided that we were not going to allow our dreams to die. We knew that we had heard from God, and Satan was not going to steal our dream. Then, as we aggressively laid hold on God's promises again, we saw a supernatural restoration in our ministry.

I want to challenge you today to recapture your dream. You may have lost it at some time. We're all human. We all make mistakes. However, if you have sown toward the fulfillment of that dream, then don't you dare let go of what is rightfully yours. There is a harvest out there with your name on it. It is time for you to claim it as yours. Don't let the devil take it away from you.

The reason I can teach you about recapturing your dreams is that I've let go of mine a time or two. However, I have never allowed myself to quit. That is not an option to me.

The Lord said to me one time: *You planted your seed for your dream then you let the weeds grow up around it. The seed is still in the ground. It's still there. Now, get the weeds off of your seed. You are entitled to your harvest. If you'll refuse to give it up, I'll bring it to pass.*

Can you identify with that? I'm sure that you can. If God will bring my dream to pass, then He'll do it for you, too.

REVIVE US...THAT THY PEOPLE MAY REJOICE

The psalmist wrote, "Wilt thou not revive us again: that thy people may rejoice in thee?" (Ps. 85:6). Revival restores your joy. Revival restores the fun in your Christianity. Revival restores the excitement about waiting for your dream and watching it come to pass, even if it's happening little by little.

I remember years ago when God first spoke to my wife and me about going into our own ministry. I was so excited when I formed my Evangelistic Association. I drove to the post office every day with joy and opened my box, only to find that there was nothing there. Day after day I went only to find that no one had written to me, no one had sent me an offering, and it seemed that no one knew our ministry existed.

I'll never forget the day I drove up to that post office and found my first letter in my box. Another minister had sent me one hundred dollars! That offering reminded me that I really did have a dream from God. It caused me to have a greater confidence that my dream would come to pass.

God wants you to have that same excitement. He wants to restore your joy. He wants you to finish your course. The apostle Paul said, when facing opposition:

> *But none of these things move me, neither count I my life dear unto myself, so that I might finish my course with joy, and the ministry, which I have received of the Lord Jesus, to testify the gospel of the grace of God.*
>
> Acts 20:24

No matter how things look on the outside, you cannot be moved by what you see. Refusing to be moved by your circumstances is the way that you will fulfill your dream and finish your course with joy.

SEVEN CHARACTERISTICS OF A GOD-GIVEN DREAM

Let's take a look at the life of Moses and see what his God-given dream produced in him.

> *And the Lord said, I have surely seen the affliction of my people which are in Egypt, and have heard their*

cry by reason of their taskmasters; for I know their sorrows;

And I am come down to deliver them out of the hand of the Egyptians, and to bring them up out of that land unto a good land and a large, unto a land flowing with milk and honey; unto the place of the Canaanites, and the Hittites, and the Amorites, and the Perizzites, and the Hivites, and the Jebusites.

Now therefore, behold, the cry of the children of Israel is come unto me: and I have also seen the oppression wherewith the Egyptians oppress them.

Come now therefore, and I will send thee unto Pharaoh, that thou mayest bring forth my people the children of Israel out of Egypt.

And Moses said unto God, Who am I, that I should go unto Pharaoh, and that I should bring forth the children of Israel out of Egypt?

Exodus 3:7-11

1. A God-given dream establishes identity.

Moses asked God, "Who am I?" He's seeking identity. God wanted Moses to become established in his identity in Him. Your identity in God is vital to fulfilling your dream. It lets you know that God is the author of your dream and not you.

2. A God-given dream establishes authority.

Exodus 3:13-14 says:

> *And Moses said unto God, Behold, when I come unto the children of Israel, and shall say unto them, The God of your fathers hath sent me unto you; and they shall say to me, What is his name? what shall I say unto them?*
>
> *And God said unto Moses, I AM THAT I AM: and he said, Thus shalt thou say unto the children of Israel, I AM hath sent me unto you.*

All the authority that you need to fulfill your dream is in God—the I AM is the One who backs you.

3. A God-given dream establishes credibility.

This can be seen as the story of Moses continues in the fourth chapter of Exodus:

And Moses answered and said, But, behold, they will not believe me, nor hearken unto my voice: for they will say, The Lord hath not appeared unto thee.

And the Lord said unto him, What is that in thine hand? And he said, A rod.

And he said, Cast it on the ground. And he cast it on the ground, and it became a serpent; and Moses fled from before it.

And the Lord said unto Moses, Put forth thine hand, and take it by the tail. And he put forth his hand, and caught it, and it became a rod in his hand:

That they may believe that the Lord God of their fathers, the God of Abraham, the God of Isaac, and the God of Jacob, hath appeared unto thee.

Exodus 4:1-5

Here, Moses is looking for credibility. When you have a God-given dream and you know your divine destiny, some people will ask what right you have to do what you are doing. They may be skeptical of the fact that you are endeavoring to accomplish something well beyond your natural means. They may even criticize you for surpassing their expectations of you. However, when you have a dream, whether you have the praise of man or not, you know you have credibility with God. He is the One who gave you your dream.

4. A God-given dream establishes ability.

Moses had a habit of talking about his inability, but when God gave him a dream, it established ability. When you have a dream, then like Moses, you will also have God's divine ability to get the job done.

5. A God-given dream establishes courage.

Exodus 4:18 says:

> *And Moses went and returned to Jethro his father in law, and said unto him, Let me go, I pray thee, and return unto my brethren which are in Egypt, and see whether they be yet alive. And Jethro said to Moses, Go in peace.*

After a long discussion in which Moses was extremely honest with God, he finally accepted the dream that God had for him. Therefore, verse 18 tells us, "And Moses went." The dream established within Moses the courage to do what God had told him to do. Courage enables us to go after what God says is ours.

6. A God-given dream establishes boldness.

In Exodus 5:1-2 we see his first confrontation with Pharaoh:

And afterward Moses and Aaron went in, and told Pharaoh, Thus saith the Lord God of Israel, Let my people go, that they may hold a feast unto me in the wilderness.

And Pharaoh said, Who is the Lord, that I should obey his voice to let Israel go? I know not the Lord, neither will I let Israel go.

Moses is no longer fearful. He's not afraid to step out in faith.

This is not the same man who had been saying, "I am not…" or "I can't do…." This man is now boldly demanding that Pharaoh let God's people go!

7. A God-given dream establishes perseverance.

You will see throughout the story of Moses that he had to continually approach and confront Pharaoh. He had developed perseverance. He had what I like to call a no-quit attitude. He would not give up until his dream had become reality.

God is looking for believers who are not afraid to persevere. He is looking for people who are willing to talk more about what God can do than about what they cannot do. God's divine ability is available to anyone who is willing to take that step of faith to follow after what He has called them to and refuse to quit.

Are you willing to take that step? If so, then get ready to see your dream come to pass.

ABOUT THE AUTHOR

Dr. Jerry Savelle was an average, blue-collar man who struggled and needed God's help. While he considered himself a "nobody," when he became a believer, God told him not to worry about it because He was a master at making champions out of nobodies. God took Dr. Savelle from being a constant quitter to a man who knew how to stand on the Word of God until victory was experienced. Because of the life-changing combination of God's faithfulness and Dr. Savelle's "no quit" attitude, his life was totally different than it was fifty years ago.

Since 1969, Dr. Savelle traveled the world, teaching people how to win in life. Dr. Savelle ministered in over thirty-five hundred churches in over forty nations and had overseas offices in the United Kingdom, Australia, Canada, and South Africa, as well as numerous Bible schools in several nations.

God used Dr. Savelle to inspire people worldwide to take hold of the promises of God and become the winners in life that God has called them to be, and to become a testimony to His faithfulness.

He hosted the Jerry Savelle Ministries television broadcast in two hundred countries worldwide. He was the author of more than seventy books, including his bestsellers: *If Satan Can't Steal Your Joy, He Can't Keep Your Goods* and *Called to Battle, Destined to Win*. He and his wife, Carolyn, also served as founding pastors of Heritage of Faith Christian Center in Crowley, Texas.

OTHER BOOKS BY JERRY SAVELLE

If Satan Can't Steal Your Dreams…He Can't Control Your Destiny

Expect the Extraordinary

The Established Heart

A Right Mental Attitude

Sharing Jesus Effectively

The Nature of Faith

Force of Joy

God's Provision for Healing

Victory & Success Are Yours!

Purged by Fire

You Can Have Abundant Life

Are You Tired of Sowing Much?

Don't Let Go of Your Dreams

Faith Building Daily Devotionals

Honoring Your Heritage of Faith

Turning Your Adversity into Victory
How to Overcome Financial Famine
Leaving the Tears Behind
You're Somebody Special to God

Visit our website or contact us for
a complete list of resources
by Jerry Savelle.
Jerry Savelle Ministries
P. O. Box 748
Crowley, Texas 76036
www.jsmi.org

Please include your prayer requests
and comments when you write.

In the Right Hands, This Book Will Change Lives!

Most of the people who need this message will not be looking for this book. To change their lives, you need to **put a copy of this book in their hands.**

Our ministry is constantly seeking methods to find the people who need this anointed message to change their lives. **Will you help us reach these people?**

Extend this ministry by sowing three, five, ten, or *even more* books today and change people's lives for the better! Your generosity will be part of catalyzing the Great Awakening that many have been prophesying and praying for.

YOUR HOUSE OF
FAITH

Sign up for a **FREE** subscription to the Harrison House digital magazine and get excellent content delivered directly to your inbox!

harrisonhouse.com/signup

Sign up for Messages that Equip You to Walk in the Abundant Life

• Receive biblically sound and Spirit-filled encouragement to focus on and maintain your faith
• Grow in faith through biblical teachings, prayers, and other spiritual insights
• Connect with a community of believers who share your values and beliefs

Experience Fresh Teachings and Inspiration to Build Your Faith

• Deepen your understanding of God's purpose for your life
• Stay connected and inspired on your faith journey
• Learn how to grow spiritually in your walk with God

BECOME THE WINNER GOD CREATED YOU TO BE

The purpose of the Jerry Savelle Bible School is to fulfill one of God's mandates given to Dr. Jerry Savelle – MASS DISCIPLESHIP.

Jesus said, "If you abide in My word [hold fast to My teachings and live in accordance with them], you are truly My disciples". Jesus' words show us there is much more than the new birth if we want to be called His disciple.

- **EXPERIENCE A 'SCHOOL WITHOUT WALLS' ACCESSIBLE TO ALL, REGARDLESS OF LOCATION OR COMMITMENTS**

- **BUILD A SOLID FOUNDATION IN GOD'S WORD THROUGH REDEMPTIVE TRUTHS**

- **BECOME EQUIPPED WITH THE UNCOMPROMISING WORD OF GOD**

- **RECEIVE ELITE TEACHINGS THAT FOSTER PERSONAL AND SPIRITUAL GROWTH**

- **FULFILL YOUR MINISTRY CALL!**

ENROLL TODAY
JERRYSAVELLE.ORG/BIBLE-SCHOOL

SCAN THIS QR CODE NOW

JERRY SAVELLE
Ministries International

FOR ADDITIONAL INFORMATION ABOUT
JERRY SAVELLE MINISTRIES INTERNATIONAL
VISIT OUR WEBSITE

JERRYSAVELLE.ORG

JERRY SAVELLE
Ministries International

Other best-selling books by Dr. Jerry Savelle:

- *From Devastation to Restoration*
- *The Favor of God*
- *Called to Battle, Destined to Win*
- *The God of the Breakthrough*
  Will Visit Your House
- *In the Footsteps of a Prophet*
- *Prayer of Petition*

JERRYSAVELLE.ORG